Lean Accounting Best Practices Complete Self-Assessment Guide

The guidance in this Self-Assessment is based
Practices best practices and standards in business process architecture, design and quality management. The guidance is also based on the professional judgment of the individual collaborators listed in the Acknowledgments.

Notice of rights

Trademarks

Table of Contents

About The Art of Service   8

Included Resources - how to access   8
Purpose of this Self-Assessment   10
How to use the Self-Assessment   11
Lean Accounting Best Practices
Scorecard Example   13

Lean Accounting Best Practices
Scorecard   14

BEGINNING OF THE
SELF-ASSESSMENT: 15
CRITERION #1: RECOGNIZE   16

CRITERION #2: DEFINE: 28

CRITERION #3: MEASURE: 44

CRITERION #4: ANALYZE: 59

CRITERION #5: IMPROVE: 75

CRITERION #6: CONTROL: 92

CRITERION #7: SUSTAIN: 104
Lean Accounting Best Practices and Managing Projects,
Criteria for Project Managers: 130
1.0 Initiating Process Group: Lean Accounting Best Practices
                                                        131

1.1 Project Charter: Lean Accounting Best Practices   133

1.2 Stakeholder Register: Lean Accounting Best Practices 135

1.3 Stakeholder Analysis Matrix: Lean Accounting Best Practices   136

2.0 Planning Process Group: Lean Accounting Best Practices   138

2.1 Project Management Plan: Lean Accounting Best Practices   140

2.2 Scope Management Plan: Lean Accounting Best Practices   142

2.3 Requirements Management Plan: Lean Accounting Best Practices   144

2.4 Requirements Documentation: Lean Accounting Best Practices   146

2.5 Requirements Traceability Matrix: Lean Accounting Best Practices   148

2.6 Project Scope Statement: Lean Accounting Best Practices   150

2.7 Assumption and Constraint Log: Lean Accounting Best Practices   152

2.8 Work Breakdown Structure: Lean Accounting Best Practices   154

2.9 WBS Dictionary: Lean Accounting Best Practices   156

2.10 Schedule Management Plan: Lean Accounting Best Practices   159

2.11 Activity List: Lean Accounting Best Practices   161

2.12 Activity Attributes: Lean Accounting Best Practices   163

2.13 Milestone List: Lean Accounting Best Practices   165

2.14 Network Diagram: Lean Accounting Best Practices   167

2.15 Activity Resource Requirements: Lean Accounting Best
Practices   169

2.16 Resource Breakdown Structure: Lean Accounting Best
Practices   171

2.17 Activity Duration Estimates: Lean Accounting Best
Practices   173

2.18 Duration Estimating Worksheet: Lean Accounting Best
Practices   175

2.19 Project Schedule: Lean Accounting Best Practices   177

2.20 Cost Management Plan: Lean Accounting Best Practices
                                                          179

2.21 Activity Cost Estimates: Lean Accounting Best Practices
                                                          181

2.22 Cost Estimating Worksheet: Lean Accounting Best
Practices   183

2.23 Cost Baseline: Lean Accounting Best Practices   185

2.24 Quality Management Plan: Lean Accounting Best
Practices   187

2.25 Quality Metrics: Lean Accounting Best Practices   189

2.26 Process Improvement Plan: Lean Accounting Best
Practices   191

2.27 Responsibility Assignment Matrix: Lean Accounting Best Practices 193

2.28 Roles and Responsibilities: Lean Accounting Best Practices 195

2.29 Human Resource Management Plan: Lean Accounting Best Practices 197

2.30 Communications Management Plan: Lean Accounting Best Practices 199

2.31 Risk Management Plan: Lean Accounting Best Practices 201

2.32 Risk Register: Lean Accounting Best Practices 203

2.33 Probability and Impact Assessment: Lean Accounting Best Practices 205

2.34 Probability and Impact Matrix: Lean Accounting Best Practices 207

2.35 Risk Data Sheet: Lean Accounting Best Practices 209

2.36 Procurement Management Plan: Lean Accounting Best Practices 211

2.37 Source Selection Criteria: Lean Accounting Best Practices 213

2.38 Stakeholder Management Plan: Lean Accounting Best Practices 215

2.39 Change Management Plan: Lean Accounting Best Practices 217

3.0 Executing Process Group: Lean Accounting Best Practices
219

3.1 Team Member Status Report: Lean Accounting Best
Practices   221

3.2 Change Request: Lean Accounting Best Practices   223

3.3 Change Log: Lean Accounting Best Practices   225

3.4 Decision Log: Lean Accounting Best Practices   227

3.5 Quality Audit: Lean Accounting Best Practices   229

3.6 Team Directory: Lean Accounting Best Practices   232

3.7 Team Operating Agreement: Lean Accounting Best
Practices   234

3.8 Team Performance Assessment: Lean Accounting Best
Practices   236

3.9 Team Member Performance Assessment: Lean
Accounting Best Practices   238

3.10 Issue Log: Lean Accounting Best Practices   240

4.0 Monitoring and Controlling Process Group: Lean
Accounting Best Practices   242

4.1 Project Performance Report: Lean Accounting Best
Practices   244

4.2 Variance Analysis: Lean Accounting Best Practices 246

4.3 Earned Value Status: Lean Accounting Best Practices 248

4.4 Risk Audit: Lean Accounting Best Practices   250

4.5 Contractor Status Report: Lean Accounting Best Practices
252

4.6 Formal Acceptance: Lean Accounting Best Practices 254

5.0 Closing Process Group: Lean Accounting Best Practices
256

5.1 Procurement Audit: Lean Accounting Best Practices 258

5.2 Contract Close-Out: Lean Accounting Best Practices 261

5.3 Project or Phase Close-Out: Lean Accounting Best
Practices 263

5.4 Lessons Learned: Lean Accounting Best Practices 265
Index 267

About The Art of Service

The Art of Service, Business Process Architects since 2000, is dedicated to helping stakeholders achieve excellence.

Defining, designing, creating, and implementing a process to solve a stakeholders challenge or meet an objective is the most valuable role... In EVERY group, company, organization and department.

Unless you're talking a one-time, single-use project, there should be a process. Whether that process is managed and implemented by humans, AI, or a combination of the two, it needs to be designed by someone with a complex enough perspective to ask the right questions.

Someone capable of asking the right questions and step back and say, 'What are we really trying to accomplish here? And is there a different way to look at it?'

With The Art of Service's Standard Requirements Self-Assessments, we empower people who can do just that — whether their title is marketer, entrepreneur, manager, salesperson, consultant, Business Process Manager, executive assistant, IT Manager, CIO etc... —they are the people who rule the future. They are people who watch the process as it happens, and ask the right questions to make the process work better.

Contact us when you need any support with this Self-Assessment and any help with templates, blue-prints and examples of standard documents you might need:

http://theartofservice.com
service@theartofservice.com

Included Resources - how to access

Included with your purchase of the book is the Lean Accounting

Best Practices Self-Assessment Spreadsheet Dashboard which contains all questions and Self-Assessment areas and auto-generates insights, graphs, and project RACI planning - all with examples to get you started right away.

How? Simply send an email to
access@theartofservice.com
with this books' title in the subject to get the Lean Accounting Best Practices Self Assessment Tool right away.

You will receive the following contents with New and Updated specific criteria:

- The latest quick edition of the book in PDF

- The latest complete edition of the book in PDF, which criteria correspond to the criteria in...

- The Self-Assessment Excel Dashboard, and...

- Example pre-filled Self-Assessment Excel Dashboard to get familiar with results generation

- In-depth specific Checklists covering the topic

- Project management checklists and templates to assist with implementation

INCLUDES LIFETIME SELF ASSESSMENT UPDATES

Every self assessment comes with Lifetime Updates and Lifetime Free Updated Books. Lifetime Updates is an industry-first feature which allows you to receive verified self assessment updates, ensuring you always have the most accurate information at your fingertips.

Get it now- you will be glad you did - do it now, before you forget.

Send an email to **access@theartofservice.com** with this books' title in the subject to get the Lean Accounting Best Practices Self Assessment Tool right away.

Purpose of this Self-Assessment

This Self-Assessment has been developed to improve understanding of the requirements and elements of Lean Accounting Best Practices, based on best practices and standards in business process architecture, design and quality management.

It is designed to allow for a rapid Self-Assessment to determine how closely existing management practices and procedures correspond to the elements of the Self-Assessment.

The criteria of requirements and elements of Lean Accounting Best Practices have been rephrased in the format of a Self-Assessment questionnaire, with a seven-criterion scoring system, as explained in this document.

In this format, even with limited background knowledge of Lean Accounting Best Practices, a manager can quickly review existing operations to determine how they measure up to the standards. This in turn can serve as the starting point of a 'gap analysis' to identify management tools or system elements that might usefully be implemented in the organization to help improve overall performance.

How to use the Self-Assessment

On the following pages are a series of questions to identify to what extent your Lean Accounting Best Practices initiative is complete in comparison to the requirements set in standards.

To facilitate answering the questions, there is a space in front of each question to enter a score on a scale of '1' to '5'.

1 Strongly Disagree

2 Disagree

3 Neutral

4 Agree

5 Strongly Agree

Read the question and rate it with the following in front of mind:

**'In my belief,
the answer to this question is clearly defined'.**

There are two ways in which you can choose to interpret this statement;
1. how aware are you that the answer to the question is clearly defined
2. for more in-depth analysis you can choose to gather evidence and confirm the answer to the question. This obviously will take more time, most Self-Assessment users opt for the first way to interpret the question and dig deeper later on based on the outcome of the overall Self-Assessment.

A score of '1' would mean that the answer is not clear at all, where a '5' would mean the answer is crystal clear and defined. Leave emtpy when the question is not applicable or you don't want to answer it, you can skip it without affecting your score. Write your score in the space provided.

After you have responded to all the appropriate statements in each section, compute your average score for that section, using the formula provided, and round to the nearest tenth. Then transfer to the corresponding spoke in the Lean Accounting Best Practices Scorecard on the second next page of the Self-Assessment.

Your completed Lean Accounting Best Practices Scorecard will give you a clear presentation of which Lean Accounting Best Practices areas need attention.

Lean Accounting Best Practices
Scorecard Example

Example of how the finalized Scorecard can look like:

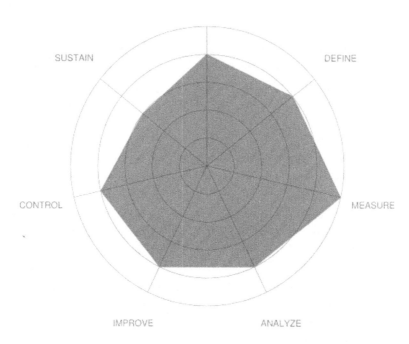

Lean Accounting Best Practices Scorecard

Your Scores:

BEGINNING OF THE SELF-ASSESSMENT:

CRITERION #1: RECOGNIZE

INTENT: Be aware of the need for change. Recognize that there is an unfavorable variation, problem or symptom.

In my belief, the answer to this question is clearly defined:

5 Strongly Agree

4 Agree

3 Neutral

2 Disagree

1 Strongly Disagree

1. How do you take a forward-looking perspective in identifying Lean accounting best practices research related to market response and models?
<--- Score

2. Have you identified your Lean accounting best practices key performance indicators?
<--- Score

3. How do you recognize an objection?
<--- Score

4. Does Lean accounting best practices create potential expectations in other areas that need to be recognized and considered?
<--- Score

5. Did you miss any major Lean accounting best practices issues?
<--- Score

6. Are you dealing with any of the same issues today as yesterday? What can you do about this?
<--- Score

7. What creative shifts do you need to take?
<--- Score

8. What is the recognized need?
<--- Score

9. Who else hopes to benefit from it?
<--- Score

10. What is the problem and/or vulnerability?
<--- Score

11. Why is this needed?
<--- Score

12. How much are sponsors, customers, partners, stakeholders involved in Lean accounting best practices? In other words, what are the risks, if Lean accounting best practices does not deliver successfully?

<--- Score

13. How do you recognize an Lean accounting best practices objection?
<--- Score

14. How do you assess your Lean accounting best practices workforce capability and capacity needs, including skills, competencies, and staffing levels?
<--- Score

15. What are the stakeholder objectives to be achieved with Lean accounting best practices?
<--- Score

16. What prevents you from making the changes you know will make you a more effective Lean accounting best practices leader?
<--- Score

17. How can auditing be a preventative security measure?
<--- Score

18. Who needs to know?
<--- Score

19. Are losses recognized in a timely manner?
<--- Score

20. What Lean accounting best practices events should you attend?
<--- Score

21. Do you know what you need to know about Lean accounting best practices?

<--- Score

22. Think about the people you identified for your Lean accounting best practices project and the project responsibilities you would assign to them, what kind of training do you think they would need to perform these responsibilities effectively?
<--- Score

23. Why the need?
<--- Score

24. Is the quality assurance team identified?
<--- Score

25. What information do users need?
<--- Score

26. Do you need different information or graphics?
<--- Score

27. Are there recognized Lean accounting best practices problems?
<--- Score

28. What is the problem or issue?
<--- Score

29. Which issues are too important to ignore?
<--- Score

30. Whom do you really need or want to serve?
<--- Score

31. Would you recognize a threat from the inside?
<--- Score

32. To what extent does each concerned units management team recognize Lean accounting best practices as an effective investment?
<--- Score

33. Are there any specific expectations or concerns about the Lean accounting best practices team, Lean accounting best practices itself?
<--- Score

34. Where do you need to exercise leadership?
<--- Score

35. What do you need to start doing?
<--- Score

36. What vendors make products that address the Lean accounting best practices needs?
<--- Score

37. Who needs what information?
<--- Score

38. Are there any revenue recognition issues?
<--- Score

39. Are there Lean accounting best practices problems defined?
<--- Score

40. For your Lean accounting best practices project, identify and describe the business environment, is there more than one layer to the business environment?
<--- Score

41. Will it solve real problems?
<--- Score

42. What activities does the governance board need to consider?
<--- Score

43. Are controls defined to recognize and contain problems?
<--- Score

44. What situation(s) led to this Lean accounting best practices Self Assessment?
<--- Score

45. As a sponsor, customer or management, how important is it to meet goals, objectives?
<--- Score

46. How does it fit into your organizational needs and tasks?
<--- Score

47. What does Lean accounting best practices success mean to the stakeholders?
<--- Score

48. Who needs to know about Lean accounting best practices?
<--- Score

49. How are you going to measure success?
<--- Score

50. What are the Lean accounting best practices

resources needed?
<--- Score

51. What is the smallest subset of the problem you can usefully solve?
<--- Score

52. Where is training needed?
<--- Score

53. Do you need to avoid or amend any Lean accounting best practices activities?
<--- Score

54. Which needs are not included or involved?
<--- Score

55. Will new equipment/products be required to facilitate Lean accounting best practices delivery, for example is new software needed?
<--- Score

56. What are the expected benefits of Lean accounting best practices to the stakeholder?
<--- Score

57. How many trainings, in total, are needed?
<--- Score

58. What do employees need in the short term?
<--- Score

59. Does the problem have ethical dimensions?
<--- Score

60. Are problem definition and motivation clearly

presented?
<--- Score

61. Are there regulatory / compliance issues?
<--- Score

62. What training and capacity building actions are needed to implement proposed reforms?
<--- Score

63. What are the minority interests and what amount of minority interests can be recognized?
<--- Score

64. Is it needed?
<--- Score

65. Does your organization need more Lean accounting best practices education?
<--- Score

66. Are your goals realistic? Do you need to redefine your problem? Perhaps the problem has changed or maybe you have reached your goal and need to set a new one?
<--- Score

67. What else needs to be measured?
<--- Score

68. Do you recognize Lean accounting best practices achievements?
<--- Score

69. Will a response program recognize when a crisis occurs and provide some level of response?

<--- Score

70. Looking at each person individually – does every one have the qualities which are needed to work in this group?
<--- Score

71. Who should resolve the Lean accounting best practices issues?
<--- Score

72. To what extent would your organization benefit from being recognized as a award recipient?
<--- Score

73. What Lean accounting best practices coordination do you need?
<--- Score

74. What are the clients issues and concerns?
<--- Score

75. Who needs budgets?
<--- Score

76. What Lean accounting best practices problem should be solved?
<--- Score

77. How are the Lean accounting best practices's objectives aligned to the group's overall stakeholder strategy?
<--- Score

78. When a Lean accounting best practices manager recognizes a problem, what options are available?

<--- Score

79. Is it clear when you think of the day ahead of you what activities and tasks you need to complete?
<--- Score

80. What are your needs in relation to Lean accounting best practices skills, labor, equipment, and markets?
<--- Score

81. What needs to be done?
<--- Score

82. What is the extent or complexity of the Lean accounting best practices problem?
<--- Score

83. What is the Lean accounting best practices problem definition? What do you need to resolve?
<--- Score

84. What Lean accounting best practices capabilities do you need?
<--- Score

85. Who defines the rules in relation to any given issue?
<--- Score

86. Are employees recognized for desired behaviors?
<--- Score

87. What needs to stay?
<--- Score

88. What should be considered when identifying available resources, constraints, and deadlines?
<--- Score

89. Are employees recognized or rewarded for performance that demonstrates the highest levels of integrity?
<--- Score

90. What problems are you facing and how do you consider Lean accounting best practices will circumvent those obstacles?
<--- Score

91. Which information does the Lean accounting best practices business case need to include?
<--- Score

92. What resources or support might you need?
<--- Score

93. How do you identify the kinds of information that you will need?
<--- Score

94. Is the need for organizational change recognized?
<--- Score

95. What would happen if Lean accounting best practices weren't done?
<--- Score

96. Do you have/need 24-hour access to key personnel?
<--- Score

97. What extra resources will you need?
<--- Score

98. Can management personnel recognize the monetary benefit of Lean accounting best practices?
<--- Score

99. Will Lean accounting best practices deliverables need to be tested and, if so, by whom?
<--- Score

Add up total points for this section:
_ _ _ _ _ = Total points for this section

Divided by: _ _ _ _ _ _ (number of statements answered) = _ _ _ _ _ _
Average score for this section

Transfer your score to the Lean accounting best practices Index at the beginning of the Self-Assessment.

CRITERION #2: DEFINE:

INTENT: Formulate the stakeholder problem. Define the problem, needs and objectives.

In my belief, the answer to this question is clearly defined:

5 Strongly Agree

4 Agree

3 Neutral

2 Disagree

1 Strongly Disagree

1. What scope do you want your strategy to cover?
<--- Score

2. Are the Lean accounting best practices requirements complete?
<--- Score

3. What are the core elements of the Lean accounting best practices business case?

<--- Score

4. What specifically is the problem? Where does it occur? When does it occur? What is its extent?
<--- Score

5. Has a project plan, Gantt chart, or similar been developed/completed?
<--- Score

6. What sort of initial information to gather?
<--- Score

7. Are all requirements met?
<--- Score

8. Are audit criteria, scope, frequency and methods defined?
<--- Score

9. Who is gathering information?
<--- Score

10. What gets examined?
<--- Score

11. Is scope creep really all bad news?
<--- Score

12. Is there regularly 100% attendance at the team meetings? If not, have appointed substitutes attended to preserve cross-functionality and full representation?
<--- Score

13. Are required metrics defined, what are they?

<--- Score

14. What is the definition of Lean accounting best practices excellence?
<--- Score

15. Do you have a Lean accounting best practices success story or case study ready to tell and share?
<--- Score

16. Has the direction changed at all during the course of Lean accounting best practices? If so, when did it change and why?
<--- Score

17. What key stakeholder process output measure(s) does Lean accounting best practices leverage and how?
<--- Score

18. Has anyone else (internal or external to the group) attempted to solve this problem or a similar one before? If so, what knowledge can be leveraged from these previous efforts?
<--- Score

19. Who are the Lean accounting best practices improvement team members, including Management Leads and Coaches?
<--- Score

20. Has the improvement team collected the 'voice of the customer' (obtained feedback – qualitative and quantitative)?
<--- Score

21. Have all basic functions of Lean accounting best practices been defined?
<--- Score

22. Are roles and responsibilities formally defined?
<--- Score

23. Is Lean accounting best practices linked to key stakeholder goals and objectives?
<--- Score

24. Do you all define Lean accounting best practices in the same way?
<--- Score

25. How have you defined all Lean accounting best practices requirements first?
<--- Score

26. Is the Lean accounting best practices scope manageable?
<--- Score

27. Is special Lean accounting best practices user knowledge required?
<--- Score

28. What customer feedback methods were used to solicit their input?
<--- Score

29. Has/have the customer(s) been identified?
<--- Score

30. How can the value of Lean accounting best practices be defined?

<--- Score

31. Who approved the Lean accounting best practices scope?
<--- Score

32. Is there a completed SIPOC representation, describing the Suppliers, Inputs, Process, Outputs, and Customers?
<--- Score

33. How do you manage changes in Lean accounting best practices requirements?
<--- Score

34. Do you have organizational privacy requirements?
<--- Score

35. How did the Lean accounting best practices manager receive input to the development of a Lean accounting best practices improvement plan and the estimated completion dates/times of each activity?
<--- Score

36. What is a worst-case scenario for losses?
<--- Score

37. Is the improvement team aware of the different versions of a process: what they think it is vs. what it actually is vs. what it should be vs. what it could be?
<--- Score

38. How do you manage unclear Lean accounting best practices requirements?
<--- Score

39. Scope of sensitive information?
<--- Score

40. When is/was the Lean accounting best practices start date?
<--- Score

41. In what way can you redefine the criteria of choice clients have in your category in your favor?
<--- Score

42. Where can you gather more information?
<--- Score

43. What is the worst case scenario?
<--- Score

44. What are the tasks and definitions?
<--- Score

45. Does the scope remain the same?
<--- Score

46. How do you manage scope?
<--- Score

47. Are there different segments of customers?
<--- Score

48. What are the compelling stakeholder reasons for embarking on Lean accounting best practices?
<--- Score

49. What are the rough order estimates on cost savings/opportunities that Lean accounting best practices brings?

<--- Score

50. What information do you gather?
<--- Score

51. What is the scope of the Lean accounting best practices effort?
<--- Score

52. What are (control) requirements for Lean accounting best practices Information?
<--- Score

53. How do you build the right business case?
<--- Score

54. What is the context?
<--- Score

55. How do you gather the stories?
<--- Score

56. How does the Lean accounting best practices manager ensure against scope creep?
<--- Score

57. How will variation in the actual durations of each activity be dealt with to ensure that the expected Lean accounting best practices results are met?
<--- Score

58. What are the dynamics of the communication plan?
<--- Score

59. What Lean accounting best practices services do

you require?
<--- Score

60. Is there a completed, verified, and validated high-level 'as is' (not 'should be' or 'could be') stakeholder process map?
<--- Score

61. Has everyone on the team, including the team leaders, been properly trained?
<--- Score

62. What are the requirements for audit information?
<--- Score

63. How do you think the partners involved in Lean accounting best practices would have defined success?
<--- Score

64. Who defines (or who defined) the rules and roles?
<--- Score

65. Are task requirements clearly defined?
<--- Score

66. How would you define the culture at your organization, how susceptible is it to Lean accounting best practices changes?
<--- Score

67. What are the Roles and Responsibilities for each team member and its leadership? Where is this documented?
<--- Score

68. What intelligence can you gather?
<--- Score

69. Is there a clear Lean accounting best practices case definition?
<--- Score

70. What are the record-keeping requirements of Lean accounting best practices activities?
<--- Score

71. Are there any constraints known that bear on the ability to perform Lean accounting best practices work? How is the team addressing them?
<--- Score

72. How do you keep key subject matter experts in the loop?
<--- Score

73. How is the team tracking and documenting its work?
<--- Score

74. What constraints exist that might impact the team?
<--- Score

75. Are different versions of process maps needed to account for the different types of inputs?
<--- Score

76. How often are the team meetings?
<--- Score

77. What information should you gather?

<--- Score

78. What are the Lean accounting best practices use cases?
<--- Score

79. If substitutes have been appointed, have they been briefed on the Lean accounting best practices goals and received regular communications as to the progress to date?
<--- Score

80. How will the Lean accounting best practices team and the group measure complete success of Lean accounting best practices?
<--- Score

81. Is the team equipped with available and reliable resources?
<--- Score

82. What sources do you use to gather information for a Lean accounting best practices study?
<--- Score

83. Is the current 'as is' process being followed? If not, what are the discrepancies?
<--- Score

84. Has the Lean accounting best practices work been fairly and/or equitably divided and delegated among team members who are qualified and capable to perform the work? Has everyone contributed?
<--- Score

85. The political context: who holds power?

<--- Score

86. What happens if Lean accounting best practices's scope changes?
<--- Score

87. What baselines are required to be defined and managed?
<--- Score

88. Is there any additional Lean accounting best practices definition of success?
<--- Score

89. Are customer(s) identified and segmented according to their different needs and requirements?
<--- Score

90. How and when will the baselines be defined?
<--- Score

91. What is the scope of Lean accounting best practices?
<--- Score

92. Is Lean accounting best practices required?
<--- Score

93. Has a team charter been developed and communicated?
<--- Score

94. What is in the scope and what is not in scope?
<--- Score

95. Has a Lean accounting best practices requirement

not been met?
<--- Score

96. Have the customer needs been translated into specific, measurable requirements? How?
<--- Score

97. Have specific policy objectives been defined?
<--- Score

98. Has your scope been defined?
<--- Score

99. Are the Lean accounting best practices requirements testable?
<--- Score

100. How was the 'as is' process map developed, reviewed, verified and validated?
<--- Score

101. Is data collected and displayed to better understand customer(s) critical needs and requirements.
<--- Score

102. What is the scope of the Lean accounting best practices work?
<--- Score

103. Have all of the relationships been defined properly?
<--- Score

104. What is out of scope?
<--- Score

105. What would be the goal or target for a Lean accounting best practices's improvement team?
<--- Score

106. How do you hand over Lean accounting best practices context?
<--- Score

107. When is the estimated completion date?
<--- Score

108. Do the problem and goal statements meet the SMART criteria (specific, measurable, attainable, relevant, and time-bound)?
<--- Score

109. How would you define Lean accounting best practices leadership?
<--- Score

110. Is there a critical path to deliver Lean accounting best practices results?
<--- Score

111. What knowledge or experience is required?
<--- Score

112. Will a Lean accounting best practices production readiness review be required?
<--- Score

113. What critical content must be communicated – who, what, when, where, and how?
<--- Score

114. What is in scope?
<--- Score

115. Is Lean accounting best practices currently on schedule according to the plan?
<--- Score

116. How do you gather Lean accounting best practices requirements?
<--- Score

117. Who is gathering Lean accounting best practices information?
<--- Score

118. What scope to assess?
<--- Score

119. Has a high-level 'as is' process map been completed, verified and validated?
<--- Score

120. What defines best in class?
<--- Score

121. Are accountability and ownership for Lean accounting best practices clearly defined?
<--- Score

122. Is there a Lean accounting best practices management charter, including stakeholder case, problem and goal statements, scope, milestones, roles and responsibilities, communication plan?
<--- Score

123. When are meeting minutes sent out? Who is on

the distribution list?

<--- Score

124. What Lean accounting best practices requirements should be gathered?

<--- Score

125. Are approval levels defined for contracts and supplements to contracts?

<--- Score

126. Is the Lean accounting best practices scope complete and appropriately sized?

<--- Score

127. Is the work to date meeting requirements?

<--- Score

128. What is the scope?

<--- Score

129. Is the scope of Lean accounting best practices defined?

<--- Score

130. Does the team have regular meetings?

<--- Score

131. How are consistent Lean accounting best practices definitions important?

<--- Score

132. How do you gather requirements?

<--- Score

133. What system do you use for gathering Lean

accounting best practices information?
<--- Score

134. Is the team adequately staffed with the desired cross-functionality? If not, what additional resources are available to the team?
<--- Score

135. What is out-of-scope initially?
<--- Score

136. What is the definition of success?
<--- Score

137. What are the boundaries of the scope? What is in bounds and what is not? What is the start point? What is the stop point?
<--- Score

Add up total points for this section:
_____ = Total points for this section

Divided by: _____ (number of statements answered) = _____
Average score for this section

Transfer your score to the Lean accounting best practices Index at the beginning of the Self-Assessment.

CRITERION #3: MEASURE:

INTENT: Gather the correct data.
Measure the current performance and
evolution of the situation.

In my belief, the answer to this
question is clearly defined:

5 Strongly Agree

4 Agree

3 Neutral

2 Disagree

1 Strongly Disagree

1. What would be a real cause for concern?
<--- Score

2. What are the uncertainties surrounding estimates
of impact?
<--- Score

3. What are you verifying?
<--- Score

4. Are there competing Lean accounting best practices priorities?
<--- Score

5. Do you have a flow diagram of what happens?
<--- Score

6. What are the costs and benefits?
<--- Score

7. What disadvantage does this cause for the user?
<--- Score

8. Where is it measured?
<--- Score

9. What causes mismanagement?
<--- Score

10. What does verifying compliance entail?
<--- Score

11. How can you reduce costs?
<--- Score

12. What users will be impacted?
<--- Score

13. What is the cost of rework?
<--- Score

14. How do you measure variability?
<--- Score

15. Does a Lean accounting best practices

quantification method exist?
<--- Score

16. What are your primary costs, revenues, assets?
<--- Score

17. How do you verify the Lean accounting best practices requirements quality?
<--- Score

18. How can a Lean accounting best practices test verify your ideas or assumptions?
<--- Score

19. What are the strategic priorities for this year?
<--- Score

20. How will costs be allocated?
<--- Score

21. What is the root cause(s) of the problem?
<--- Score

22. At what cost?
<--- Score

23. Are supply costs steady or fluctuating?
<--- Score

24. Have design-to-cost goals been established?
<--- Score

25. How will you measure success?
<--- Score

26. Are missed Lean accounting best practices

opportunities costing your organization money?
<--- Score

27. Do you verify that corrective actions were taken?
<--- Score

28. Do the benefits outweigh the costs?
<--- Score

29. How can you manage cost down?
<--- Score

30. What measurements are possible, practicable and meaningful?
<--- Score

31. How are measurements made?
<--- Score

32. How do you prevent mis-estimating cost?
<--- Score

33. Why a Lean accounting best practices focus?
<--- Score

34. How much does it cost?
<--- Score

35. Why do you expend time and effort to implement measurement, for whom?
<--- Score

36. What is your decision requirements diagram?
<--- Score

37. How will success or failure be measured?

<--- Score

38. How do you measure lifecycle phases?
<--- Score

39. What are the costs of delaying Lean accounting best practices action?
<--- Score

40. What is the cause of any Lean accounting best practices gaps?
<--- Score

41. Among the Lean accounting best practices product and service cost to be estimated, which is considered hardest to estimate?
<--- Score

42. When should you bother with diagrams?
<--- Score

43. Which Lean accounting best practices impacts are significant?
<--- Score

44. How can you reduce the costs of obtaining inputs?
<--- Score

45. What does losing customers cost your organization?
<--- Score

46. Who should receive measurement reports?
<--- Score

47. What harm might be caused?

<--- Score

48. What is an unallowable cost?
<--- Score

49. How is the value delivered by Lean accounting best practices being measured?
<--- Score

50. Are indirect costs charged to the Lean accounting best practices program?
<--- Score

51. How frequently do you verify your Lean accounting best practices strategy?
<--- Score

52. What methods are feasible and acceptable to estimate the impact of reforms?
<--- Score

53. How is progress measured?
<--- Score

54. Are you able to realize any cost savings?
<--- Score

55. What are your operating costs?
<--- Score

56. How is performance measured?
<--- Score

57. What relevant entities could be measured?
<--- Score

58. How do you verify performance?
<--- Score

59. Did you tackle the cause or the symptom?
<--- Score

60. Which measures and indicators matter?
<--- Score

61. Are you aware of what could cause a problem?
<--- Score

62. How will measures be used to manage and adapt?
<--- Score

63. How can you measure Lean accounting best practices in a systematic way?
<--- Score

64. Do you have an issue in getting priority?
<--- Score

65. How do you measure efficient delivery of Lean accounting best practices services?
<--- Score

66. Are you taking your company in the direction of better and revenue or cheaper and cost?
<--- Score

67. What is the total cost related to deploying Lean accounting best practices, including any consulting or professional services?
<--- Score

68. What are the Lean accounting best practices key

cost drivers?

<--- Score

69. What are the types and number of measures to use?

<--- Score

70. Are there any easy-to-implement alternatives to Lean accounting best practices? Sometimes other solutions are available that do not require the cost implications of a full-blown project?

<--- Score

71. What is the Lean accounting best practices business impact?

<--- Score

72. What is the total fixed cost?

<--- Score

73. What do you measure and why?

<--- Score

74. Are the Lean accounting best practices benefits worth its costs?

<--- Score

75. How do you verify your resources?

<--- Score

76. What are the costs of reform?

<--- Score

77. How frequently do you track Lean accounting best practices measures?

<--- Score

78. Do you aggressively reward and promote the people who have the biggest impact on creating excellent Lean accounting best practices services/products?
<--- Score

79. What causes extra work or rework?
<--- Score

80. How to cause the change?
<--- Score

81. Is there an opportunity to verify requirements?
<--- Score

82. What is your Lean accounting best practices quality cost segregation study?
<--- Score

83. Does management have the right priorities among projects?
<--- Score

84. How do you verify and develop ideas and innovations?
<--- Score

85. What are your key Lean accounting best practices organizational performance measures, including key short and longer-term financial measures?
<--- Score

86. How do you quantify and qualify impacts?
<--- Score

87. Which costs should be taken into account?
<--- Score

88. What does a Test Case verify?
<--- Score

89. What do people want to verify?
<--- Score

90. How do you control the overall costs of your work processes?
<--- Score

91. Who pays the cost?
<--- Score

92. When a disaster occurs, who gets priority?
<--- Score

93. How can you measure the performance?
<--- Score

94. How long to keep data and how to manage retention costs?
<--- Score

95. What are the estimated costs of proposed changes?
<--- Score

96. Will Lean accounting best practices have an impact on current business continuity, disaster recovery processes and/or infrastructure?
<--- Score

97. Where is the cost?

<--- Score

98. Who is involved in verifying compliance?
<--- Score

99. What would it cost to replace your technology?
<--- Score

100. Are actual costs in line with budgeted costs?
<--- Score

101. Do you effectively measure and reward individual and team performance?
<--- Score

102. Are the units of measure consistent?
<--- Score

103. What happens if cost savings do not materialize?
<--- Score

104. How will you measure your Lean accounting best practices effectiveness?
<--- Score

105. Are Lean accounting best practices vulnerabilities categorized and prioritized?
<--- Score

106. How do you verify the authenticity of the data and information used?
<--- Score

107. How does the focus on right-designing value stream work flow impact enterprise cost management?

<--- Score

108. Is the cost worth the Lean accounting best practices effort ?
<--- Score

109. How do you aggregate measures across priorities?
<--- Score

110. How will effects be measured?
<--- Score

111. What is measured? Why?
<--- Score

112. Have you made assumptions about the shape of the future, particularly its impact on your customers and competitors?
<--- Score

113. What potential environmental factors impact the Lean accounting best practices effort?
<--- Score

114. How are you verifying it?
<--- Score

115. What are hidden Lean accounting best practices quality costs?
<--- Score

116. When are costs are incurred?
<--- Score

117. What are your customers expectations and

measures?
<--- Score

118. What could cause delays in the schedule?
<--- Score

119. What does your operating model cost?
<--- Score

120. Why do the measurements/indicators matter?
<--- Score

121. Has a cost center been established?
<--- Score

122. What causes innovation to fail or succeed in your organization?
<--- Score

123. How do your measurements capture actionable Lean accounting best practices information for use in exceeding your customers expectations and securing your customers engagement?
<--- Score

124. What evidence is there and what is measured?
<--- Score

125. What tests verify requirements?
<--- Score

126. What are the Lean accounting best practices investment costs?
<--- Score

127. What can be used to verify compliance?

<--- Score

128. What could cause you to change course?
<--- Score

129. What are the costs?
<--- Score

130. Does the Lean accounting best practices task fit the client's priorities?
<--- Score

131. How do you verify Lean accounting best practices completeness and accuracy?
<--- Score

132. How are costs allocated?
<--- Score

133. How do you measure success?
<--- Score

134. Are the measurements objective?
<--- Score

135. Are there measurements based on task performance?
<--- Score

136. What drives O&M cost?
<--- Score

Add up total points for this section:
_____ = Total points for this section

Divided by: _____ (number of

statements answered) = _____
Average score for this section

Transfer your score to the Lean
accounting best practices Index at the
beginning of the Self-Assessment.

CRITERION #4: ANALYZE:

INTENT: Analyze causes, assumptions and hypotheses.

In my belief, the answer to this question is clearly defined:

5 Strongly Agree

4 Agree

3 Neutral

2 Disagree

1 Strongly Disagree

1. Is the final output clearly identified?
<--- Score

2. Who will facilitate the team and process?
<--- Score

3. Has data output been validated?
<--- Score

4. Were Pareto charts (or similar) used to portray the

'heavy hitters' (or key sources of variation)?
<--- Score

5. How will the data be checked for quality?
<--- Score

6. Which Lean accounting best practices data should be retained?
<--- Score

7. Are all staff in core Lean accounting best practices subjects Highly Qualified?
<--- Score

8. What do you need to qualify?
<--- Score

9. Do you, as a leader, bounce back quickly from setbacks?
<--- Score

10. Identify an operational issue in your organization, for example, could a particular task be done more quickly or more efficiently by Lean accounting best practices?
<--- Score

11. Was a detailed process map created to amplify critical steps of the 'as is' stakeholder process?
<--- Score

12. What training and qualifications will you need?
<--- Score

13. Who gets your output?
<--- Score

14. What qualifications do Lean accounting best practices leaders need?
<--- Score

15. Record-keeping requirements flow from the records needed as inputs, outputs, controls and for transformation of a Lean accounting best practices process, are the records needed as inputs to the Lean accounting best practices process available?
<--- Score

16. Was a cause-and-effect diagram used to explore the different types of causes (or sources of variation)?
<--- Score

17. What are the disruptive Lean accounting best practices technologies that enable your organization to radically change your business processes?
<--- Score

18. Where is Lean accounting best practices data gathered?
<--- Score

19. An organizationally feasible system request is one that considers the mission, goals and objectives of the organization, key questions are: is the Lean accounting best practices solution request practical and will it solve a problem or take advantage of an opportunity to achieve company goals?
<--- Score

20. How is the way you as the leader think and process information affecting your organizational culture?
<--- Score

21. What were the financial benefits resulting from any 'ground fruit or low-hanging fruit' (quick fixes)?
<--- Score

22. Do several people in different organizational units assist with the Lean accounting best practices process?
<--- Score

23. Is the performance gap determined?
<--- Score

24. Do your leaders quickly bounce back from setbacks?
<--- Score

25. What, related to, Lean accounting best practices processes does your organization outsource?
<--- Score

26. How does the organization define, manage, and improve its Lean accounting best practices processes?
<--- Score

27. What did the team gain from developing a sub-process map?
<--- Score

28. What are the best opportunities for value improvement?
<--- Score

29. What are your best practices for minimizing Lean accounting best practices project risk, while demonstrating incremental value and quick wins

throughout the Lean accounting best practices project lifecycle?
<--- Score

30. What process should you select for improvement?
<--- Score

31. Were there any improvement opportunities identified from the process analysis?
<--- Score

32. How was the detailed process map generated, verified, and validated?
<--- Score

33. How is the Lean accounting best practices Value Stream Mapping managed?
<--- Score

34. What quality tools were used to get through the analyze phase?
<--- Score

35. What Lean accounting best practices data do you gather or use now?
<--- Score

36. What is your organizations process which leads to recognition of value generation?
<--- Score

37. What is the Value Stream Mapping?
<--- Score

38. Is there a strict change management process?
<--- Score

39. Is the required Lean accounting best practices data gathered?
<--- Score

40. How do you identify specific Lean accounting best practices investment opportunities and emerging trends?
<--- Score

41. What controls do you have in place to protect data?
<--- Score

42. What were the crucial 'moments of truth' on the process map?
<--- Score

43. Is pre-qualification of suppliers carried out?
<--- Score

44. What are the necessary qualifications?
<--- Score

45. What kind of crime could a potential new hire have committed that would not only not disqualify him/her from being hired by your organization, but would actually indicate that he/she might be a particularly good fit?
<--- Score

46. What are the personnel training and qualifications required?
<--- Score

47. How difficult is it to qualify what Lean accounting

best practices ROI is?
<--- Score

48. How do your work systems and key work processes relate to and capitalize on your core competencies?
<--- Score

49. What is your organizations system for selecting qualified vendors?
<--- Score

50. What are the processes for audit reporting and management?
<--- Score

51. What is the output?
<--- Score

52. What are your current levels and trends in key measures or indicators of Lean accounting best practices product and process performance that are important to and directly serve your customers? How do these results compare with the performance of your competitors and other organizations with similar offerings?
<--- Score

53. Is there an established change management process?
<--- Score

54. What Lean accounting best practices data will be collected?
<--- Score

55. Are you missing Lean accounting best practices opportunities?
<--- Score

56. Do you have the authority to produce the output?
<--- Score

57. What data do you need to collect?
<--- Score

58. What tools were used to narrow the list of possible causes?
<--- Score

59. Who qualifies to gain access to data?
<--- Score

60. Is the gap/opportunity displayed and communicated in financial terms?
<--- Score

61. Were any designed experiments used to generate additional insight into the data analysis?
<--- Score

62. How do you measure the operational performance of your key work systems and processes, including productivity, cycle time, and other appropriate measures of process effectiveness, efficiency, and innovation?
<--- Score

63. How is Lean accounting best practices data gathered?
<--- Score

64. What systems/processes must you excel at?
<--- Score

65. Are all team members qualified for all tasks?
<--- Score

66. Have the problem and goal statements been updated to reflect the additional knowledge gained from the analyze phase?
<--- Score

67. Where is the data coming from to measure compliance?
<--- Score

68. How do you ensure that the Lean accounting best practices opportunity is realistic?
<--- Score

69. What is the Lean accounting best practices Driver?
<--- Score

70. Who is involved in the management review process?
<--- Score

71. How can risk management be tied procedurally to process elements?
<--- Score

72. What does the data say about the performance of the stakeholder process?
<--- Score

73. Who will gather what data?
<--- Score

74. What methods do you use to gather Lean accounting best practices data?
<--- Score

75. How has the Lean accounting best practices data been gathered?
<--- Score

76. Are your outputs consistent?
<--- Score

77. What types of data do your Lean accounting best practices indicators require?
<--- Score

78. Is the suppliers process defined and controlled?
<--- Score

79. Who is involved with workflow mapping?
<--- Score

80. Do your employees have the opportunity to do what they do best everyday?
<--- Score

81. How will corresponding data be collected?
<--- Score

82. Have you defined which data is gathered how?
<--- Score

83. What are your Lean accounting best practices processes?
<--- Score

84. What are the revised rough estimates of the financial savings/opportunity for Lean accounting best practices improvements?
<--- Score

85. What Lean accounting best practices metrics are outputs of the process?
<--- Score

86. What Lean accounting best practices data should be managed?
<--- Score

87. What conclusions were drawn from the team's data collection and analysis? How did the team reach these conclusions?
<--- Score

88. What qualifications are necessary?
<--- Score

89. What is the complexity of the output produced?
<--- Score

90. What qualifications are needed?
<--- Score

91. What information qualified as important?
<--- Score

92. What is the cost of poor quality as supported by the team's analysis?
<--- Score

93. How do mission and objectives affect the Lean accounting best practices processes of your

organization?
<--- Score

94. How many input/output points does it require?
<--- Score

95. What are the Lean accounting best practices
design outputs?
<--- Score

96. How do you promote understanding that
opportunity for improvement is not criticism of the
status quo, or the people who created the status quo?
<--- Score

97. Think about some of the processes you undertake
within your organization, which do you own?
<--- Score

98. Where can you get qualified talent today?
<--- Score

99. What internal processes need improvement?
<--- Score

100. What process improvements will be needed?
<--- Score

101. How do you implement and manage your
work processes to ensure that they meet design
requirements?
<--- Score

102. What Lean accounting best practices data should
be collected?
<--- Score

103. Is data and process analysis, root cause analysis and quantifying the gap/opportunity in place?
<--- Score

104. What are your key performance measures or indicators and in-process measures for the control and improvement of your Lean accounting best practices processes?
<--- Score

105. What is the oversight process?
<--- Score

106. Is the Lean accounting best practices process severely broken such that a re-design is necessary?
<--- Score

107. How will the Lean accounting best practices data be captured?
<--- Score

108. What data is gathered?
<--- Score

109. Has an output goal been set?
<--- Score

110. Do quality systems drive continuous improvement?
<--- Score

111. What resources go in to get the desired output?
<--- Score

112. Think about the functions involved in your Lean

accounting best practices project, what processes flow from these functions?
<--- Score

113. What successful thing are you doing today that may be blinding you to new growth opportunities?
<--- Score

114. What output to create?
<--- Score

115. What are evaluation criteria for the output?
<--- Score

116. What qualifies as competition?
<--- Score

117. What other jobs or tasks affect the performance of the steps in the Lean accounting best practices process?
<--- Score

118. Who owns what data?
<--- Score

119. How do you use Lean accounting best practices data and information to support organizational decision making and innovation?
<--- Score

120. How is data used for program management and improvement?
<--- Score

121. What are your outputs?
<--- Score

122. Can you add value to the current Lean accounting best practices decision-making process (largely qualitative) by incorporating uncertainty modeling (more quantitative)?
<--- Score

123. Are Lean accounting best practices changes recognized early enough to be approved through the regular process?
<--- Score

124. What will drive Lean accounting best practices change?
<--- Score

125. What are your current levels and trends in key Lean accounting best practices measures or indicators of product and process performance that are important to and directly serve your customers?
<--- Score

126. Do your contracts/agreements contain data security obligations?
<--- Score

127. When should a process be art not science?
<--- Score

128. What tools were used to generate the list of possible causes?
<--- Score

129. How are outputs preserved and protected?
<--- Score

130. A compounding model resolution with available relevant data can often provide insight towards a solution methodology; which Lean accounting best practices models, tools and techniques are necessary?
<--- Score

131. What qualifications and skills do you need?
<--- Score

132. Is there any way to speed up the process?
<--- Score

Add up total points for this section:
_ _ _ _ _ = Total points for this section

Divided by: _ _ _ _ _ _ (number of statements answered) = _ _ _ _ _ _
Average score for this section

Transfer your score to the Lean accounting best practices Index at the beginning of the Self-Assessment.

CRITERION #5: IMPROVE:

INTENT: Develop a practical solution. Innovate, establish and test the solution and to measure the results.

In my belief, the answer to this question is clearly defined:

5 Strongly Agree

4 Agree

3 Neutral

2 Disagree

1 Strongly Disagree

1. Who should make the Lean accounting best practices decisions?
<--- Score

2. How are Lean accounting best practices risks managed?
<--- Score

3. Does a good decision guarantee a good outcome?

<--- Score

4. For decision problems, how do you develop a decision statement?
<--- Score

5. What improvements have been achieved?
<--- Score

6. Explorations of the frontiers of Lean accounting best practices will help you build influence, improve Lean accounting best practices, optimize decision making, and sustain change, what is your approach?
<--- Score

7. Was a pilot designed for the proposed solution(s)?
<--- Score

8. What area needs the greatest improvement?
<--- Score

9. Are risk triggers captured?
<--- Score

10. At what point will vulnerability assessments be performed once Lean accounting best practices is put into production (e.g., ongoing Risk Management after implementation)?
<--- Score

11. What tools were used to tap into the creativity and encourage 'outside the box' thinking?
<--- Score

12. Are you assessing Lean accounting best practices and risk?

<--- Score

13. What were the criteria for evaluating a Lean accounting best practices pilot?
<--- Score

14. What strategies for Lean accounting best practices improvement are successful?
<--- Score

15. Risk events: what are the things that could go wrong?
<--- Score

16. How do you manage and improve your Lean accounting best practices work systems to deliver customer value and achieve organizational success and sustainability?
<--- Score

17. How do you improve Lean accounting best practices service perception, and satisfaction?
<--- Score

18. Do the viable solutions scale to future needs?
<--- Score

19. What to do with the results or outcomes of measurements?
<--- Score

20. Who manages Lean accounting best practices risk?
<--- Score

21. Will the controls trigger any other risks?
<--- Score

22. What lessons, if any, from a pilot were incorporated into the design of the full-scale solution?
<--- Score

23. Would you develop a Lean accounting best practices Communication Strategy?
<--- Score

24. Can you integrate quality management and risk management?
<--- Score

25. How do you measure progress and evaluate training effectiveness?
<--- Score

26. How do you manage Lean accounting best practices risk?
<--- Score

27. What resources are required for the improvement efforts?
<--- Score

28. Who will be responsible for documenting the Lean accounting best practices requirements in detail?
<--- Score

29. What practices helps your organization to develop its capacity to recognize patterns?
<--- Score

30. What criteria will you use to assess your Lean accounting best practices risks?
<--- Score

31. What are the Lean accounting best practices security risks?
<--- Score

32. What can you do to improve?
<--- Score

33. How can you improve Lean accounting best practices?
<--- Score

34. What are the expected Lean accounting best practices results?
<--- Score

35. How will you know that a change is an improvement?
<--- Score

36. What communications are necessary to support the implementation of the solution?
<--- Score

37. How do you improve productivity?
<--- Score

38. Can you identify any significant risks or exposures to Lean accounting best practices third- parties (vendors, service providers, alliance partners etc) that concern you?
<--- Score

39. Is the Lean accounting best practices documentation thorough?
<--- Score

40. What does the 'should be' process map/design look like?
<--- Score

41. What actually has to improve and by how much?
<--- Score

42. How do you decide how much to remunerate an employee?
<--- Score

43. Are events managed to resolution?
<--- Score

44. Is supporting Lean accounting best practices documentation required?
<--- Score

45. Who controls the risk?
<--- Score

46. Who will be using the results of the measurement activities?
<--- Score

47. How will you know that you have improved?
<--- Score

48. Which of the recognised risks out of all risks can be most likely transferred?
<--- Score

49. How do you keep improving Lean accounting best practices?
<--- Score

50. Have you achieved Lean accounting best practices improvements?
<--- Score

51. How can the phases of Lean accounting best practices development be identified?
<--- Score

52. In the past few months, what is the smallest change you have made that has had the biggest positive result? What was it about that small change that produced the large return?
<--- Score

53. What do you want to improve?
<--- Score

54. What tools were most useful during the improve phase?
<--- Score

55. How is knowledge sharing about risk management improved?
<--- Score

56. What is Lean accounting best practices risk?
<--- Score

57. How significant is the improvement in the eyes of the end user?
<--- Score

58. What current systems have to be understood and/or changed?
<--- Score

59. How do you mitigate Lean accounting best practices risk?
<--- Score

60. Lean accounting best practices risk decisions: whose call Is It?
<--- Score

61. What tools were used to evaluate the potential solutions?
<--- Score

62. Is there a small-scale pilot for proposed improvement(s)? What conclusions were drawn from the outcomes of a pilot?
<--- Score

63. What are the concrete Lean accounting best practices results?
<--- Score

64. Risk Identification: What are the possible risk events your organization faces in relation to Lean accounting best practices?
<--- Score

65. For estimation problems, how do you develop an estimation statement?
<--- Score

66. What is the team's contingency plan for potential problems occurring in implementation?
<--- Score

67. Is there a high likelihood that any

recommendations will achieve their intended results?
<--- Score

68. Who manages supplier risk management in your organization?
<--- Score

69. Who makes the Lean accounting best practices decisions in your organization?
<--- Score

70. What were the underlying assumptions on the cost-benefit analysis?
<--- Score

71. Were any criteria developed to assist the team in testing and evaluating potential solutions?
<--- Score

72. What should a proof of concept or pilot accomplish?
<--- Score

73. What Lean accounting best practices improvements can be made?
<--- Score

74. What are the implications of the one critical Lean accounting best practices decision 10 minutes, 10 months, and 10 years from now?
<--- Score

75. What is the Lean accounting best practices's sustainability risk?
<--- Score

76. Are the most efficient solutions problem-specific?
<--- Score

77. What is Lean accounting best practices's impact on utilizing the best solution(s)?
<--- Score

78. Is there any other Lean accounting best practices solution?
<--- Score

79. Who are the Lean accounting best practices decision makers?
<--- Score

80. Do those selected for the Lean accounting best practices team have a good general understanding of what Lean accounting best practices is all about?
<--- Score

81. How can you better manage risk?
<--- Score

82. Risk factors: what are the characteristics of Lean accounting best practices that make it risky?
<--- Score

83. What assumptions are made about the solution and approach?
<--- Score

84. Is Lean accounting best practices documentation maintained?
<--- Score

85. Is risk periodically assessed?

<--- Score

86. How do you link measurement and risk?
<--- Score

87. Who controls key decisions that will be made?
<--- Score

88. What are your current levels and trends in key measures or indicators of workforce and leader development?
<--- Score

89. How will you know when its improved?
<--- Score

90. Who do you report Lean accounting best practices results to?
<--- Score

91. To what extent does management recognize Lean accounting best practices as a tool to increase the results?
<--- Score

92. Who are the people involved in developing and implementing Lean accounting best practices?
<--- Score

93. Are the key business and technology risks being managed?
<--- Score

94. Have you identified breakpoints and/or risk tolerances that will trigger broad consideration of a potential need for intervention or modification of

strategy?
<--- Score

95. How do you improve your likelihood of success ?
<--- Score

96. If you could go back in time five years, what decision would you make differently? What is your best guess as to what decision you're making today you might regret five years from now?
<--- Score

97. How will you measure the results?
<--- Score

98. Are the risks fully understood, reasonable and manageable?
<--- Score

99. How can you improve performance?
<--- Score

100. Why improve in the first place?
<--- Score

101. Which Lean accounting best practices solution is appropriate?
<--- Score

102. How are policy decisions made and where?
<--- Score

103. How risky is your organization?
<--- Score

104. Is the measure of success for Lean accounting

best practices understandable to a variety of people?
<--- Score

105. Where do you need Lean accounting best practices improvement?
<--- Score

106. Is the scope clearly documented?
<--- Score

107. Is the solution technically practical?
<--- Score

108. How do you measure risk?
<--- Score

109. Does the goal represent a desired result that can be measured?
<--- Score

110. What alternative responses are available to manage risk?
<--- Score

111. What is the implementation plan?
<--- Score

112. How do you measure improved Lean accounting best practices service perception, and satisfaction?
<--- Score

113. How do you go about comparing Lean accounting best practices approaches/solutions?
<--- Score

114. Is the Lean accounting best practices solution

sustainable?
<--- Score

115. Can the solution be designed and implemented within an acceptable time period?
<--- Score

116. What needs improvement? Why?
<--- Score

117. Who are the key stakeholders for the Lean accounting best practices evaluation?
<--- Score

118. What are the affordable Lean accounting best practices risks?
<--- Score

119. What attendant changes will need to be made to ensure that the solution is successful?
<--- Score

120. Who are the Lean accounting best practices decision-makers?
<--- Score

121. Do you need to do a usability evaluation?
<--- Score

122. Is the Lean accounting best practices risk managed?
<--- Score

123. How does the team improve its work?
<--- Score

124. How scalable is your Lean accounting best practices solution?
<--- Score

125. What is the risk?
<--- Score

126. What risks do you need to manage?
<--- Score

127. How is continuous improvement applied to risk management?
<--- Score

128. Do you have the optimal project management team structure?
<--- Score

129. Where do the Lean accounting best practices decisions reside?
<--- Score

130. What is the magnitude of the improvements?
<--- Score

131. Are procedures documented for managing Lean accounting best practices risks?
<--- Score

132. What tools do you use once you have decided on a Lean accounting best practices strategy and more importantly how do you choose?
<--- Score

133. Are risk management tasks balanced centrally and locally?

<--- Score

134. How will you recognize and celebrate results?
<--- Score

135. How do you define the solutions' scope?
<--- Score

136. Do you cover the five essential competencies: Communication, Collaboration,Innovation, Adaptability, and Leadership that improve an organizations ability to leverage the new Lean accounting best practices in a volatile global economy?
<--- Score

137. How do the Lean accounting best practices results compare with the performance of your competitors and other organizations with similar offerings?
<--- Score

138. Do you combine technical expertise with business knowledge and Lean accounting best practices Key topics include lifecycles, development approaches, requirements and how to make a business case?
<--- Score

139. Are decisions made in a timely manner?
<--- Score

140. What error proofing will be done to address some of the discrepancies observed in the 'as is' process?
<--- Score

Add up total points for this section:
_____ = Total points for this section

Divided by: _____ (number of
statements answered) = _____
Average score for this section

Transfer your score to the Lean
accounting best practices Index at the
beginning of the Self-Assessment.

CRITERION #6: CONTROL:

INTENT: Implement the practical solution. Maintain the performance and correct possible complications.

In my belief, the answer to this question is clearly defined:

5 Strongly Agree

4 Agree

3 Neutral

2 Disagree

1 Strongly Disagree

1. Who sets the Lean accounting best practices standards?
<--- Score

2. What quality tools were useful in the control phase?
<--- Score

3. Are you measuring, monitoring and predicting Lean accounting best practices activities to optimize

operations and profitability, and enhancing outcomes?

<--- Score

4. What are customers monitoring?

<--- Score

5. What should the next improvement project be that is related to Lean accounting best practices?

<--- Score

6. What do you measure to verify effectiveness gains?

<--- Score

7. What Lean accounting best practices standards are applicable?

<--- Score

8. How do your controls stack up?

<--- Score

9. Can you adapt and adjust to changing Lean accounting best practices situations?

<--- Score

10. Has the Lean accounting best practices value of standards been quantified?

<--- Score

11. What is the best design framework for Lean accounting best practices organization now that, in a post industrial-age if the top-down, command and control model is no longer relevant?

<--- Score

12. How do you plan for the cost of succession?

<--- Score

13. Against what alternative is success being measured?
<--- Score

14. What do your reports reflect?
<--- Score

15. Is there documentation that will support the successful operation of the improvement?
<--- Score

16. Will your goals reflect your program budget?
<--- Score

17. Are the planned controls in place?
<--- Score

18. What do you stand for--and what are you against?
<--- Score

19. Act/Adjust: What Do you Need to Do Differently?
<--- Score

20. How do you spread information?
<--- Score

21. Is there a documented and implemented monitoring plan?
<--- Score

22. How widespread is its use?
<--- Score

23. Do the Lean accounting best practices decisions

you make today help people and the planet tomorrow?

<--- Score

24. Implementation Planning: is a pilot needed to test the changes before a full roll out occurs?

<--- Score

25. Does a troubleshooting guide exist or is it needed?

<--- Score

26. How do you select, collect, align, and integrate Lean accounting best practices data and information for tracking daily operations and overall organizational performance, including progress relative to strategic objectives and action plans?

<--- Score

27. What can you control?

<--- Score

28. What adjustments to the strategies are needed?

<--- Score

29. Who has control over resources?

<--- Score

30. Who controls critical resources?

<--- Score

31. Is new knowledge gained imbedded in the response plan?

<--- Score

32. Is reporting being used or needed?

<--- Score

33. Will existing staff require re-training, for example, to learn new business processes?
<--- Score

34. How is Lean accounting best practices project cost planned, managed, monitored?
<--- Score

35. Is a response plan in place for when the input, process, or output measures indicate an 'out-of-control' condition?
<--- Score

36. Will the team be available to assist members in planning investigations?
<--- Score

37. Will any special training be provided for results interpretation?
<--- Score

38. Are documented procedures clear and easy to follow for the operators?
<--- Score

39. What should you measure to verify efficiency gains?
<--- Score

40. How will the day-to-day responsibilities for monitoring and continual improvement be transferred from the improvement team to the process owner?
<--- Score

41. What key inputs and outputs are being measured on an ongoing basis?
<--- Score

42. Are pertinent alerts monitored, analyzed and distributed to appropriate personnel?
<--- Score

43. How will input, process, and output variables be checked to detect for sub-optimal conditions?
<--- Score

44. How can you best use all of your knowledge repositories to enhance learning and sharing?
<--- Score

45. What is the control/monitoring plan?
<--- Score

46. Is there a recommended audit plan for routine surveillance inspections of Lean accounting best practices's gains?
<--- Score

47. Are there documented procedures?
<--- Score

48. How will you measure your QA plan's effectiveness?
<--- Score

49. Is a response plan established and deployed?
<--- Score

50. How do you monitor usage and cost?
<--- Score

51. Are the planned controls working?
<--- Score

52. Has the improved process and its steps been standardized?
<--- Score

53. Is there a control plan in place for sustaining improvements (short and long-term)?
<--- Score

54. Does the response plan contain a definite closed loop continual improvement scheme (e.g., plan-do-check-act)?
<--- Score

55. What other areas of the group might benefit from the Lean accounting best practices team's improvements, knowledge, and learning?
<--- Score

56. How do you establish and deploy modified action plans if circumstances require a shift in plans and rapid execution of new plans?
<--- Score

57. Who will be in control?
<--- Score

58. What is your theory of human motivation, and how does your compensation plan fit with that view?
<--- Score

59. What are the critical parameters to watch?
<--- Score

60. How do you plan on providing proper recognition and disclosure of supporting companies?
<--- Score

61. In the case of a Lean accounting best practices project, the criteria for the audit derive from implementation objectives, an audit of a Lean accounting best practices project involves assessing whether the recommendations outlined for implementation have been met, can you track that any Lean accounting best practices project is implemented as planned, and is it working?
<--- Score

62. Does job training on the documented procedures need to be part of the process team's education and training?
<--- Score

63. How likely is the current Lean accounting best practices plan to come in on schedule or on budget?
<--- Score

64. How will new or emerging customer needs/ requirements be checked/communicated to orient the process toward meeting the new specifications and continually reducing variation?
<--- Score

65. How will the process owner and team be able to hold the gains?
<--- Score

66. What other systems, operations, processes, and infrastructures (hiring practices, staffing, training,

incentives/rewards, metrics/dashboards/scorecards,
etc.) need updates, additions, changes, or deletions
in order to facilitate knowledge transfer and
improvements?
<--- Score

67. Is knowledge gained on process shared and
institutionalized?
<--- Score

68. Who is going to spread your message?
<--- Score

69. What is the recommended frequency of auditing?
<--- Score

70. Have new or revised work instructions resulted?
<--- Score

71. Who is the Lean accounting best practices process
owner?
<--- Score

72. How is change control managed?
<--- Score

73. How will Lean accounting best practices decisions
be made and monitored?
<--- Score

74. What are the known security controls?
<--- Score

75. Do you monitor the effectiveness of your Lean
accounting best practices activities?
<--- Score

76. What are you attempting to measure/monitor?
<--- Score

77. What is your plan to assess your security risks?
<--- Score

78. You may have created your quality measures at a time when you lacked resources, technology wasn't up to the required standard, or low service levels were the industry norm. Have those circumstances changed?
<--- Score

79. What are your results for key measures or indicators of the accomplishment of your Lean accounting best practices strategy and action plans, including building and strengthening core competencies?
<--- Score

80. Are controls in place and consistently applied?
<--- Score

81. Is there a transfer of ownership and knowledge to process owner and process team tasked with the responsibilities.
<--- Score

82. How will report readings be checked to effectively monitor performance?
<--- Score

83. Are suggested corrective/restorative actions indicated on the response plan for known causes to problems that might surface?

<--- Score

84. How do you encourage people to take control and responsibility?
<--- Score

85. How might the group capture best practices and lessons learned so as to leverage improvements?
<--- Score

86. What are the key elements of your Lean accounting best practices performance improvement system, including your evaluation, organizational learning, and innovation processes?
<--- Score

87. Does the Lean accounting best practices performance meet the customer's requirements?
<--- Score

88. Is there a Lean accounting best practices Communication plan covering who needs to get what information when?
<--- Score

89. Are operating procedures consistent?
<--- Score

90. Is the Lean accounting best practices test/ monitoring cost justified?
<--- Score

91. How will the process owner verify improvement in present and future sigma levels, process capabilities?
<--- Score

92. Is there a standardized process?
<--- Score

93. Does Lean accounting best practices appropriately measure and monitor risk?
<--- Score

94. Do you monitor the Lean accounting best practices decisions made and fine tune them as they evolve?
<--- Score

95. Are new process steps, standards, and documentation ingrained into normal operations?
<--- Score

Add up total points for this section:
_ _ _ _ _ = Total points for this section

Divided by: _ _ _ _ _ _ (number of statements answered) = _ _ _ _ _ _
Average score for this section

Transfer your score to the Lean accounting best practices Index at the beginning of the Self-Assessment.

CRITERION #7: SUSTAIN:

INTENT: Retain the benefits.

In my belief, the answer to this question is clearly defined:

5 Strongly Agree

4 Agree

3 Neutral

2 Disagree

1 Strongly Disagree

1. Who will manage the integration of tools?
<--- Score

2. If you had to rebuild your organization without any traditional competitive advantages (i.e., no killer technology, promising research, innovative product/ service delivery model, etcetera), how would your people have to approach their work and collaborate together in order to create the necessary conditions for success?
<--- Score

3. What potential megatrends could make your business model obsolete?
<--- Score

4. Why will customers want to buy your organizations products/services?
<--- Score

5. What does your signature ensure?
<--- Score

6. What is it like to work for you?
<--- Score

7. What are your most important goals for the strategic Lean accounting best practices objectives?
<--- Score

8. How can you negotiate Lean accounting best practices successfully with a stubborn boss, an irate client, or a deceitful coworker?
<--- Score

9. Do you have an implicit bias for capital investments over people investments?
<--- Score

10. Are you relevant? Will you be relevant five years from now? Ten?
<--- Score

11. Are you paying enough attention to the partners your company depends on to succeed?
<--- Score

12. Were lessons learned captured and communicated?
<--- Score

13. What information is critical to your organization that your executives are ignoring?
<--- Score

14. Can you maintain your growth without detracting from the factors that have contributed to your success?
<--- Score

15. Are you maintaining a past–present–future perspective throughout the Lean accounting best practices discussion?
<--- Score

16. If you had to leave your organization for a year and the only communication you could have with employees/colleagues was a single paragraph, what would you write?
<--- Score

17. Are you / should you be revolutionary or evolutionary?
<--- Score

18. Did anyone think Sarbanes would be as far reaching or as controversial as it has been?
<--- Score

19. What are the barriers to increased Lean accounting best practices production?
<--- Score

20. How much contingency will be available in the budget?
<--- Score

21. Who have you, as a company, historically been when you've been at your best?
<--- Score

22. How do you transition from the baseline to the target?
<--- Score

23. How do you ensure that implementations of Lean accounting best practices products are done in a way that ensures safety?
<--- Score

24. Which functions and people interact with the supplier and or customer?
<--- Score

25. Is there a work around that you can use?
<--- Score

26. What new services of functionality will be implemented next with Lean accounting best practices ?
<--- Score

27. Who are the key stakeholders?
<--- Score

28. What should you stop doing?
<--- Score

29. Are you making progress, and are you making

progress as Lean accounting best practices leaders?
<--- Score

30. How do you keep the momentum going?
<--- Score

31. How do you make it meaningful in connecting
Lean accounting best practices with what users do
day-to-day?
<--- Score

32. In a project to restructure Lean accounting best
practices outcomes, which stakeholders would you
involve?
<--- Score

33. What have you done to protect your business from
competitive encroachment?
<--- Score

34. What is your competitive advantage?
<--- Score

35. How do you track customer value, profitability
or financial return, organizational success, and
sustainability?
<--- Score

36. What are the gaps in your knowledge and
experience?
<--- Score

37. Are you using a design thinking approach
and integrating Innovation, Lean accounting best
practices Experience, and Brand Value?
<--- Score

38. Operational - will it work?
<--- Score

39. Which models, tools and techniques are necessary?
<--- Score

40. How is implementation research currently incorporated into each of your goals?
<--- Score

41. How can you become the company that would put you out of business?
<--- Score

42. How do you create buy-in?
<--- Score

43. What are specific Lean accounting best practices rules to follow?
<--- Score

44. If you find that you havent accomplished one of the goals for one of the steps of the Lean accounting best practices strategy, what will you do to fix it?
<--- Score

45. How does Lean accounting best practices integrate with other stakeholder initiatives?
<--- Score

46. Who do we want your customers to become?
<--- Score

47. What are internal and external Lean accounting

best practices relations?

<--- Score

48. How do customers see your organization?

<--- Score

49. What is an unauthorized commitment?

<--- Score

50. Where can you break convention?

<--- Score

51. How do you deal with Lean accounting best practices changes?

<--- Score

52. Is Lean accounting best practices dependent on the successful delivery of a current project?

<--- Score

53. What threat is Lean accounting best practices addressing?

<--- Score

54. Is maximizing Lean accounting best practices protection the same as minimizing Lean accounting best practices loss?

<--- Score

55. What business benefits will Lean accounting best practices goals deliver if achieved?

<--- Score

56. What did you miss in the interview for the worst hire you ever made?

<--- Score

57. What one word do you want to own in the minds of your customers, employees, and partners?
<--- Score

58. Who do you want your customers to become?
<--- Score

59. What management system can you use to leverage the Lean accounting best practices experience, ideas, and concerns of the people closest to the work to be done?
<--- Score

60. How do you proactively clarify deliverables and Lean accounting best practices quality expectations?
<--- Score

61. What was the last experiment you ran?
<--- Score

62. If you weren't already in this business, would you enter it today? And if not, what are you going to do about it?
<--- Score

63. What are the usability implications of Lean accounting best practices actions?
<--- Score

64. Is Lean accounting best practices realistic, or are you setting yourself up for failure?
<--- Score

65. Is a Lean accounting best practices breakthrough on the horizon?

<--- Score

66. What is the source of the strategies for Lean accounting best practices strengthening and reform?
<--- Score

67. How much does Lean accounting best practices help?
<--- Score

68. What Lean accounting best practices modifications can you make work for you?
<--- Score

69. How do you foster innovation?
<--- Score

70. Why should people listen to you?
<--- Score

71. How will you motivate the stakeholders with the least vested interest?
<--- Score

72. Who will determine interim and final deadlines?
<--- Score

73. What is your Lean accounting best practices strategy?
<--- Score

74. What may be the consequences for the performance of an organization if all stakeholders are not consulted regarding Lean accounting best practices?
<--- Score

75. Have benefits been optimized with all key stakeholders?
<--- Score

76. Whom among your colleagues do you trust, and for what?
<--- Score

77. How do you cross-sell and up-sell your Lean accounting best practices success?
<--- Score

78. What is the overall business strategy?
<--- Score

79. How do you determine the key elements that affect Lean accounting best practices workforce satisfaction, how are these elements determined for different workforce groups and segments?
<--- Score

80. What is the recommended frequency of auditing?
<--- Score

81. How will you insure seamless interoperability of Lean accounting best practices moving forward?
<--- Score

82. What happens when a new employee joins the organization?
<--- Score

83. Is the impact that Lean accounting best practices has shown?
<--- Score

84. What is the CFOs role in implementing a lean business strategy?

<--- Score

85. Are there any activities that you can take off your to do list?

<--- Score

86. If you do not follow, then how to lead?

<--- Score

87. Why is Lean accounting best practices important for you now?

<--- Score

88. What is the big Lean accounting best practices idea?

<--- Score

89. What is your BATNA (best alternative to a negotiated agreement)?

<--- Score

90. Are the criteria for selecting recommendations stated?

<--- Score

91. What trouble can you get into?

<--- Score

92. Who is on the team?

<--- Score

93. What have been your experiences in defining long range Lean accounting best practices goals?

<--- Score

94. If you got fired and a new hire took your place, what would she do different?
<--- Score

95. Can you do all this work?
<--- Score

96. Do you have enough freaky customers in your portfolio pushing you to the limit day in and day out?
<--- Score

97. Think of your Lean accounting best practices project, what are the main functions?
<--- Score

98. Are your responses positive or negative?
<--- Score

99. Ask yourself: how would you do this work if you only had one staff member to do it?
<--- Score

100. Marketing budgets are tighter, consumers are more skeptical, and social media has changed forever the way we talk about Lean accounting best practices, how do you gain traction?
<--- Score

101. When information truly is ubiquitous, when reach and connectivity are completely global, when computing resources are infinite, and when a whole new set of impossibilities are not only possible, but happening, what will that do to your business?
<--- Score

102. What would have to be true for the option on the table to be the best possible choice?
<--- Score

103. Are the assumptions believable and achievable?
<--- Score

104. Is a Lean accounting best practices team work effort in place?
<--- Score

105. Will it be accepted by users?
<--- Score

106. What will be the consequences to the stakeholder (financial, reputation etc) if Lean accounting best practices does not go ahead or fails to deliver the objectives?
<--- Score

107. In the past year, what have you done (or could you have done) to increase the accurate perception of your company/brand as ethical and honest?
<--- Score

108. How will you ensure you get what you expected?
<--- Score

109. Who are your customers?
<--- Score

110. If you were responsible for initiating and implementing major changes in your organization, what steps might you take to ensure acceptance of those changes?

<--- Score

111. Who is responsible for ensuring appropriate resources (time, people and money) are allocated to Lean accounting best practices?
<--- Score

112. How likely is it that a customer would recommend your company to a friend or colleague?
<--- Score

113. What are the short and long-term Lean accounting best practices goals?
<--- Score

114. What counts that you are not counting?
<--- Score

115. Do you have the right capabilities and capacities?
<--- Score

116. What relationships among Lean accounting best practices trends do you perceive?
<--- Score

117. Who will be responsible for deciding whether Lean accounting best practices goes ahead or not after the initial investigations?
<--- Score

118. What are the rules and assumptions your industry operates under? What if the opposite were true?
<--- Score

119. What are the top 3 things at the forefront of your Lean accounting best practices agendas for the next 3

years?

<--- Score

120. What must be done well at the cell level if the value stream objectives are to be achieved?

<--- Score

121. What are you challenging?

<--- Score

122. Is there any reason to believe the opposite of my current belief?

<--- Score

123. What are current Lean accounting best practices paradigms?

<--- Score

124. Do you have past Lean accounting best practices successes?

<--- Score

125. What are the success criteria that will indicate that Lean accounting best practices objectives have been met and the benefits delivered?

<--- Score

126. What are the business goals Lean accounting best practices is aiming to achieve?

<--- Score

127. How can you incorporate support to ensure safe and effective use of Lean accounting best practices into the services that you provide?

<--- Score

128. What is the range of capabilities?
<--- Score

129. What could happen if you do not do it?
<--- Score

130. Is your basic point _____ or _____?
<--- Score

131. How do you foster the skills, knowledge, talents, attributes, and characteristics you want to have?
<--- Score

132. How will you know that the Lean accounting best practices project has been successful?
<--- Score

133. Are new benefits received and understood?
<--- Score

134. How can you become more high-tech but still be high touch?
<--- Score

135. How do you keep records, of what?
<--- Score

136. What is the overall talent health of your organization as a whole at senior levels, and for each organization reporting to a member of the Senior Leadership Team?
<--- Score

137. How do senior leaders deploy your organizations vision and values through your leadership system, to the workforce, to key suppliers and partners, and to

customers and other stakeholders, as appropriate?
<--- Score

138. Do you have the right people on the bus?
<--- Score

139. What you are going to do to affect the numbers?
<--- Score

140. What are the potential basics of Lean accounting best practices fraud?
<--- Score

141. What is something you believe that nearly no one agrees with you on?
<--- Score

142. Is there any existing Lean accounting best practices governance structure?
<--- Score

143. How do you accomplish your long range Lean accounting best practices goals?
<--- Score

144. How do you go about securing Lean accounting best practices?
<--- Score

145. Who else should you help?
<--- Score

146. How do you engage the workforce, in addition to satisfying them?
<--- Score

147. Is the Lean accounting best practices organization completing tasks effectively and efficiently?
<--- Score

148. How do you listen to customers to obtain actionable information?
<--- Score

149. What trophy do you want on your mantle?
<--- Score

150. What must you excel at?
<--- Score

151. How do you set Lean accounting best practices stretch targets and how do you get people to not only participate in setting these stretch targets but also that they strive to achieve these?
<--- Score

152. What is the craziest thing you can do?
<--- Score

153. Are all key stakeholders present at all Structured Walkthroughs?
<--- Score

154. How are you doing compared to your industry?
<--- Score

155. How long will it take to change?
<--- Score

156. Will there be any necessary staff changes (redundancies or new hires)?

<--- Score

157. Whose voice (department, ethnic group, women, older workers, etc) might you have missed hearing from in your company, and how might you amplify this voice to create positive momentum for your business?
<--- Score

158. Who is responsible for errors?
<--- Score

159. What are your personal philosophies regarding Lean accounting best practices and how do they influence your work?
<--- Score

160. Who do you think the world wants your organization to be?
<--- Score

161. In retrospect, of the projects that you pulled the plug on, what percent do you wish had been allowed to keep going, and what percent do you wish had ended earlier?
<--- Score

162. What are the essentials of internal Lean accounting best practices management?
<--- Score

163. Which Lean accounting best practices goals are the most important?
<--- Score

164. What is the purpose of Lean accounting best

practices in relation to the mission?
<--- Score

165. How do you provide a safe environment
-physically and emotionally?
<--- Score

166. Is it economical; do you have the time and
money?
<--- Score

167. What stupid rule would you most like to kill?
<--- Score

168. Do you think you know, or do you know you
know ?
<--- Score

169. What knowledge, skills and characteristics
mark a good Lean accounting best practices project
manager?
<--- Score

170. How do you lead with Lean accounting best
practices in mind?
<--- Score

171. Who, on the executive team or the board, has
spoken to a customer recently?
<--- Score

172. What role does communication play in the
success or failure of a Lean accounting best practices
project?
<--- Score

173. Do you feel that more should be done in the Lean accounting best practices area?
<--- Score

174. What would you recommend your friend do if he/she were facing this dilemma?
<--- Score

175. Instead of going to current contacts for new ideas, what if you reconnected with dormant contacts--the people you used to know? If you were going reactivate a dormant tie, who would it be?
<--- Score

176. What is a feasible sequencing of reform initiatives over time?
<--- Score

177. Do you know who is a friend or a foe?
<--- Score

178. Would you rather sell to knowledgeable and informed customers or to uninformed customers?
<--- Score

179. Are assumptions made in Lean accounting best practices stated explicitly?
<--- Score

180. What are the long-term Lean accounting best practices goals?
<--- Score

181. Why not do Lean accounting best practices?
<--- Score

182. Is your strategy driving your strategy? Or is the way in which you allocate resources driving your strategy?
<--- Score

183. How do you govern and fulfill your societal responsibilities?
<--- Score

184. How important is Lean accounting best practices to the user organizations mission?
<--- Score

185. What is effective Lean accounting best practices?
<--- Score

186. How do you assess the Lean accounting best practices pitfalls that are inherent in implementing it?
<--- Score

187. If there were zero limitations, what would you do differently?
<--- Score

188. What happens at your organization when people fail?
<--- Score

189. Are you satisfied with your current role? If not, what is missing from it?
<--- Score

190. Who will provide the final approval of Lean accounting best practices deliverables?
<--- Score

191. What is the estimated value of the project?
<--- Score

192. Have new benefits been realized?
<--- Score

193. How do you manage Lean accounting best practices Knowledge Management (KM)?
<--- Score

194. What is your question? Why?
<--- Score

195. How do you stay inspired?
<--- Score

196. To whom do you add value?
<--- Score

197. Why should you adopt a Lean accounting best practices framework?
<--- Score

198. If your company went out of business tomorrow, would anyone who doesn't get a paycheck here care?
<--- Score

199. Are you changing as fast as the world around you?
<--- Score

200. What is the funding source for this project?
<--- Score

201. Do you say no to customers for no reason?
<--- Score

202. What do we do when new problems arise?
<--- Score

203. Who is responsible for Lean accounting best practices?
<--- Score

204. Do you think Lean accounting best practices accomplishes the goals you expect it to accomplish?
<--- Score

205. Who uses your product in ways you never expected?
<--- Score

206. What happens if you do not have enough funding?
<--- Score

207. At what moment would you think; Will I get fired?
<--- Score

208. What goals did you miss?
<--- Score

209. What are strategies for increasing support and reducing opposition?
<--- Score

210. Has implementation been effective in reaching specified objectives so far?
<--- Score

211. Who is the main stakeholder, with ultimate responsibility for driving Lean accounting best

practices forward?

<--- Score

212. What is the kind of project structure that would be appropriate for your Lean accounting best practices project, should it be formal and complex, or can it be less formal and relatively simple?

<--- Score

213. What must be done well at the value stream if the strategic goals are to be achieved?

<--- Score

214. Do Lean accounting best practices rules make a reasonable demand on a users capabilities?

<--- Score

215. Why is it important to have senior management support for a Lean accounting best practices project?

<--- Score

216. What unique value proposition (UVP) do you offer?

<--- Score

217. What are the challenges?

<--- Score

Add up total points for this section:
_ _ _ _ _ = Total points for this section

Divided by: _ _ _ _ _ _ (number of statements answered) = _ _ _ _ _ _
Average score for this section

Transfer your score to the Lean

accounting best practices Index at the
beginning of the Self-Assessment.

Lean Accounting Best Practices and Managing Projects, Criteria for Project Managers:

1.0 Initiating Process Group: Lean Accounting Best Practices

1. In which Lean Accounting Best Practices project management process group is the detailed Lean Accounting Best Practices project budget created?

2. Are identified risks being monitored properly, are new risks arising during the Lean Accounting Best Practices project or are foreseen risks occurring?

3. What were the challenges that you encountered during the execution of a previous Lean Accounting Best Practices project that you would not want to repeat?

4. What communication items need improvement?

5. First of all, should any action be taken?

6. Although the Lean Accounting Best Practices project manager does not directly manage procurement and contracting activities, who does manage procurement and contracting activities in your organization then if not the PM?

7. Do you know if the Lean Accounting Best Practices project requires outside equipment or vendor resources?

8. Do you understand the communication expectations for this Lean Accounting Best Practices project?

9. What are the constraints?

10. Were resources available as planned?

11. Were decisions made in a timely manner?

12. What are the required resources?

13. For technology Lean Accounting Best Practices projects only: Are all production support stakeholders (Business unit, technical support, & user) prepared for implementation with appropriate contingency plans?

14. Do you know the Lean Accounting Best Practices projects goal, purpose and objectives?

15. Do you understand the quality and control criteria that must be achieved for successful Lean Accounting Best Practices project completion?

16. Who does what?

17. What are the short and long term implications?

18. How do you help others satisfy needs?

19. Did the Lean Accounting Best Practices project team have the right skills?

20. The Lean Accounting Best Practices project you are managing has nine stakeholders. How many channel of communications are there between corresponding stakeholders?

1.1 Project Charter: Lean Accounting Best Practices

21. Where does all this information come from?

22. Why do you need to manage scope?

23. Lean Accounting Best Practices project background: what is the primary motivation for this Lean Accounting Best Practices project?

24. For whom?

25. How much?

26. Why is it important?

27. Dependent Lean Accounting Best Practices projects: what Lean Accounting Best Practices projects must be underway or completed before this Lean Accounting Best Practices project can be successful?

28. When do you use a Lean Accounting Best Practices project Charter?

29. Who is the Lean Accounting Best Practices project Manager?

30. Who are the stakeholders?

31. Avoid costs, improve service, and/ or comply with a mandate?

32. Run it as as a startup?

33. What goes into your Lean Accounting Best Practices project Charter?

34. What ideas do you have for initial tests of change (PDSA cycles)?

35. Are you building in-house ?

36. What is the justification?

37. What is the most common tool for helping define the detail?

38. Why is a Lean Accounting Best Practices project Charter used?

39. Who ise input and support will this Lean Accounting Best Practices project require?

40. How will you know that a change is an improvement?

1.2 Stakeholder Register: Lean Accounting Best Practices

41. What is the power of the stakeholder?

42. Who is managing stakeholder engagement?

43. How should employers make voices heard?

44. What opportunities exist to provide communications?

45. How much influence do they have on the Lean Accounting Best Practices project?

46. Is your organization ready for change?

47. What are the major Lean Accounting Best Practices project milestones requiring communications or providing communications opportunities?

48. Who wants to talk about Security?

49. What & Why?

50. How will reports be created?

51. How big is the gap?

1.3 Stakeholder Analysis Matrix: Lean Accounting Best Practices

52. How are you predicting what future (work)loads will be?

53. How will the Lean Accounting Best Practices project benefit them?

54. Which conditions out of the control of the management are crucial to contribute for the achievement of the development objective?

55. Who is directly responsible for decisions on issues important to the Lean Accounting Best Practices project?

56. Who is most dependent on the resources at stake?

57. Are the required specifications for products or services changing?

58. Which conditions out of the control of the management are crucial for the sustainability of its effects?

59. Industry or lifestyle trends?

60. New USPs?

61. Cultural, attitudinal, behavioural?

62. Are there two or three that rise to the top, and a

couple that are sliding to the bottom?

63. How affected by the problem(s)?

64. What tools would help you communicate?

65. Participatory approach: how will key stakeholders participate in the Lean Accounting Best Practices project?

66. Who will be affected by the work?

67. Philosophy and values?

68. Does the stakeholder want to be involved or merely need to be informed about the Lean Accounting Best Practices project and its process?

69. Morale, commitment, leadership?

70. Processes, systems, it, communications?

2.0 Planning Process Group: Lean Accounting Best Practices

71. What input will you be required to provide the Lean Accounting Best Practices project team?

72. What is the difference between the early schedule and late schedule?

73. Is your organization showing technical capacity and leadership commitment to keep working with the Lean Accounting Best Practices project and to repeat it?

74. Explanation: is what the Lean Accounting Best Practices project intents to solve a hard question?

75. Is the schedule for the set products being met?

76. How are it Lean Accounting Best Practices projects different?

77. How should needs be met?

78. If you are late, will anybody notice?

79. What makes your Lean Accounting Best Practices project successful?

80. To what extent do the intervention objectives and strategies of the Lean Accounting Best Practices project respond to your organizations plans?

81. How well defined and documented are the Lean Accounting Best Practices project management processes you chose to use?

82. How many days can task X be late in starting without affecting the Lean Accounting Best Practices project completion date?

83. Have operating capacities been created and/or reinforced in partners?

84. What will you do?

85. What should you do next?

86. How will users learn how to use the deliverables?

87. What are the different approaches to building the WBS?

88. Will the products created live up to the necessary quality?

89. Why is it important to determine activity sequencing on Lean Accounting Best Practices projects?

2.1 Project Management Plan: Lean Accounting Best Practices

90. What went wrong?

91. What goes into your Lean Accounting Best Practices project Charter?

92. Why Change?

93. What are the known stakeholder requirements?

94. What are the assigned resources?

95. Are the proposed Lean Accounting Best Practices project purposes different than a previously authorized Lean Accounting Best Practices project?

96. What are the assumptions?

97. When is the Lean Accounting Best Practices project management plan created?

98. How do you manage time?

99. Will you add a schedule and diagram?

100. What is risk management?

101. Are there any client staffing expectations?

102. Are the existing and future without-plan conditions reasonable and appropriate?

103. Is there an incremental analysis/cost effectiveness analysis of proposed mitigation features based on an approved method and using an accepted model?

104. How do you manage integration?

105. Is there anything you would now do differently on your Lean Accounting Best Practices project based on past experience?

106. What are the training needs?

107. How do you organize the costs in the Lean Accounting Best Practices project management plan?

108. Do there need to be organizational changes?

2.2 Scope Management Plan: Lean Accounting Best Practices

109. How much money have you spent?

110. Do you have the reasons why the changes to your organizational systems and capabilities are required?

111. Are agendas created for each meeting with meeting objectives, meeting topics, invitee list, and action items from past meetings?

112. Do Lean Accounting Best Practices project teams & team members report on status / activities / progress?

113. Are assumptions being identified, recorded, analyzed, qualified and closed?

114. Are there any windfall benefits that would accrue to the Lean Accounting Best Practices project sponsor or other parties?

115. Is the schedule updated on a periodic basis?

116. Has a provision been made to reassess Lean Accounting Best Practices project risks at various Lean Accounting Best Practices project stages?

117. Organizational unit (e.g., department, team, or person) who will accept responsibility for satisfactory completion of the item?

118. Is there a formal process for updating the Lean Accounting Best Practices project baseline?

119. Are mitigation strategies identified?

120. What weaknesses do you have?

121. Are updated Lean Accounting Best Practices project time & resource estimates reasonable based on the current Lean Accounting Best Practices project stage?

122. How do you know how you are doing?

123. How do you know when you are finished?

124. Has a Lean Accounting Best Practices project Communications Plan been developed?

125. Pop quiz – what changed on Lean Accounting Best Practices project scope statement input?

126. Has process improvement efforts been completed before requirements efforts begin?

127. Have the key elements of a coherent Lean Accounting Best Practices project management strategy been established?

128. What is your organizations history in doing similar activities?

2.3 Requirements Management Plan: Lean Accounting Best Practices

129. Is the user satisfied?

130. Will you document changes to requirements?

131. To see if a requirement statement is sufficiently well-defined, read it from the developers perspective. Mentally add the phrase, call me when youre done to the end of the requirement and see if that makes you nervous. In other words, would you need additional clarification from the author to understand the requirement well enough to design and implement it?

132. Has the requirements team been instructed in the Change Control process?

133. Who will do the reporting and to whom will reports be delivered?

134. Did you provide clear and concise specifications?

135. Describe the process for rejecting the Lean Accounting Best Practices project requirements. Who has the authority to reject Lean Accounting Best Practices project requirements?

136. Who will initially review the Lean Accounting Best Practices project work or products to ensure it meets the applicable acceptance criteria?

137. Are actual resource expenditures versus planned

still acceptable?

138. How often will the reporting occur?

139. Do you have an appropriate arrangement for meetings?

140. Is the system software (non-operating system) new to the IT Lean Accounting Best Practices project team?

141. Will you have access to stakeholders when you need them?

142. What is a problem?

143. Are all the stakeholders ready for the transition into the user community?

144. Define the help desk model. who will take full responsibility?

145. Is the system software (non-operating system) new to the IT Lean Accounting Best Practices project team?

146. Subject to change control?

147. The wbs is developed as part of a joint planning session. and how do you know that youhave done this right?

148. How will bidders price evaluations be done, by deliverables, phases, or in a big bang?

2.4 Requirements Documentation: Lean Accounting Best Practices

149. What happens when requirements are wrong?

150. How much testing do you need to do to prove that your system is safe?

151. Can the requirements be checked?

152. Consistency. are there any requirements conflicts?

153. What are the acceptance criteria?

154. What is effective documentation?

155. Who is interacting with the system?

156. Is the origin of the requirement clearly stated?

157. How do you know when a Requirement is accurate enough?

158. Do technical resources exist?

159. How to document system requirements?

160. Have the benefits identified with the system being identified clearly?

161. What images does it conjure?

162. Validity. does the system provide the functions which best support the customers needs?

163. Basic work/business process; high-level, what is being touched?

164. What facilities must be supported by the system?

165. Can the requirement be changed without a large impact on other requirements?

166. What marketing channels do you want to use: e-mail, letter or sms?

167. How linear / iterative is your Requirements Gathering process (or will it be)?

168. How can you document system requirements?

2.5 Requirements Traceability Matrix: Lean Accounting Best Practices

169. How do you manage scope?

170. How will it affect the stakeholders personally in career?

171. Why use a WBS?

172. What are the chronologies, contingencies, consequences, criteria?

173. Will you use a Requirements Traceability Matrix?

174. Describe the process for approving requirements so they can be added to the traceability matrix and Lean Accounting Best Practices project work can be performed. Will the Lean Accounting Best Practices project requirements become approved in writing?

175. How small is small enough?

176. Do you have a clear understanding of all subcontracts in place?

177. What is the WBS?

178. What percentage of Lean Accounting Best Practices projects are producing traceability matrices between requirements and other work products?

179. Why do you manage scope?

180. Is there a requirements traceability process in place?

2.6 Project Scope Statement: Lean Accounting Best Practices

181. What is a process you might recommend to verify the accuracy of the research deliverable?

182. Will the Lean Accounting Best Practices project risks be managed according to the Lean Accounting Best Practices projects risk management process?

183. Has the format for tracking and monitoring schedules and costs been defined?

184. Do you anticipate new stakeholders joining the Lean Accounting Best Practices project over time?

185. Lean Accounting Best Practices project lead, team lead, solution architect?

186. Is this process communicated to the customer and team members?

187. Are the input requirements from the team members clearly documented and communicated?

188. Which risks does the Lean Accounting Best Practices project focus on?

189. Any new risks introduced or old risks impacted. Are there issues that could affect the existing requirements for the result, service, or product if the scope changes?

190. Will an issue form be in use?

191. Is there a baseline plan against which to measure progress?

192. Is the Lean Accounting Best Practices project sponsor function identified and defined?

193. What is the product of this Lean Accounting Best Practices project?

194. Is there a process (test plans, inspections, reviews) defined for verifying outputs for each task?

195. Will the qa related information be reported regularly as part of the status reporting mechanisms?

196. How often do you estimate that the scope might change, and why?

197. What is change?

198. Will tasks be marked complete only after QA has been successfully completed?

2.7 Assumption and Constraint Log: Lean Accounting Best Practices

199. Have all involved stakeholders and work groups committed to the Lean Accounting Best Practices project?

200. Can the requirements be traced to the appropriate components of the solution, as well as test scripts?

201. Contradictory information between different documents?

202. What do you audit?

203. How many Lean Accounting Best Practices project staff does this specific process affect?

204. Does the document/deliverable meet general requirements (for example, statement of work) for all deliverables?

205. Can you perform this task or activity in a more effective manner?

206. Do documented requirements exist for all critical components and areas, including technical, business, interfaces, performance, security and conversion requirements?

207. Have adequate resources been provided by management to ensure Lean Accounting Best

Practices project success?

208. Diagrams and tables are included to account for complex concepts and increase overall readability?

209. Have the scope, objectives, costs, benefits and impacts been communicated to all involved and/or impacted stakeholders and work groups?

210. Are there ways to reduce the time it takes to get something approved?

211. Is the current scope of the Lean Accounting Best Practices project substantially different than that originally defined in the approved Lean Accounting Best Practices project plan?

212. Does the system design reflect the requirements?

213. Is the steering committee active in Lean Accounting Best Practices project oversight?

214. Does a documented Lean Accounting Best Practices project organizational policy & plan (i.e. governance model) exist?

215. Should factors be unpredictable over time?

216. After observing execution of process, is it in compliance with the documented Plan?

217. What strengths do you have?

218. Are there processes in place to ensure internal consistency between the source code components?

2.8 Work Breakdown Structure: Lean Accounting Best Practices

219. Do you need another level?

220. Why is it useful?

221. When would you develop a Work Breakdown Structure?

222. What is the probability of completing the Lean Accounting Best Practices project in less that xx days?

223. Is the work breakdown structure (wbs) defined and is the scope of the Lean Accounting Best Practices project clear with assigned deliverable owners?

224. When does it have to be done?

225. Is it a change in scope?

226. Why would you develop a Work Breakdown Structure?

227. How will you and your Lean Accounting Best Practices project team define the Lean Accounting Best Practices projects scope and work breakdown structure?

228. Where does it take place?

229. How many levels?

230. What is the probability that the Lean Accounting Best Practices project duration will exceed xx weeks?

231. How far down?

232. When do you stop?

233. How big is a work-package?

234. How much detail?

235. Who has to do it?

236. Is it still viable?

2.9 WBS Dictionary: Lean Accounting Best Practices

237. Where learning is used in developing underlying budgets is there a direct relationship between anticipated learning and time phased budgets?

238. Is the work done on a work package level as described in the WBS dictionary?

239. Are data being used by managers in an effective manner to ascertain Lean Accounting Best Practices project or functional status, to identify reasons or significant variance, and to initiate appropriate corrective action?

240. Cwbs elements to be subcontracted, with identification of subcontractors?

241. Are retroactive changes to BCWS and BCWP prohibited except for correction of errors or for normal accounting adjustments?

242. Does the contractors system identify work accomplishment against the schedule plan?

243. Is the anticipated (firm and potential) business base Lean Accounting Best Practices projected in a rational, consistent manner?

244. Are management actions taken to reduce indirect costs when there are significant adverse variances?

245. Are indirect costs charged to the appropriate indirect pools and incurring organization?

246. Is all contract work included in the CWBS?

247. Is undistributed budget limited to contract effort which cannot yet be planned to CWBS elements at or below the level specified for reporting to the Government?

248. Are work packages reasonably short in time duration or do they have adequate objective indicators/milestones to minimize subjectivity of the in process work evaluation?

249. Do work packages reflect the actual way in which the work will be done and are they meaningful products or management-oriented subdivisions of a higher level element of work?

250. Are the contractors estimates of costs at completion reconcilable with cost data reported to us?

251. What is wrong with this Lean Accounting Best Practices project?

252. Do procedures specify under what circumstances replanning of open work packages may occur, and the methods to be followed?

253. Does the contractors system provide for determination of price variance by comparing planned Vs actual commitments?

254. Does the contractor require sufficient detailed planning of control accounts to constrain the application of budget initially allocated for future effort to current effort?

255. Incurrence of actual indirect costs in excess of budgets, by element of expense?

256. Knowledgeable Lean Accounting Best Practices projections of future performance?

2.10 Schedule Management Plan: Lean Accounting Best Practices

257. Are staff skills known and available for each task?

258. Are corrective actions and variances reported?

259. Is an industry recognized mechanized support tool(s) being used for Lean Accounting Best Practices project scheduling & tracking?

260. Sensitivity analysis?

261. Cost / benefit analysis?

262. Does the schedule have reasonable float?

263. Is there an approved case?

264. What happens if a warning is triggered?

265. Have all documents been archived in a Lean Accounting Best Practices project repository for each release?

266. Is a payment system in place with proper reviews and approvals?

267. Are written status reports provided on a designated frequent basis?

268. Are the predecessor and successor relationships accurate?

269. Are the constraints or deadlines associated with the task accurate?

270. Identify the amount of schedule variation that triggers a warning. What happens if a warning is triggered?

271. Is documentation created for communication with the suppliers and Vendors?

272. Are there any activities or deliverables being added or gold-plated that could be dropped or scaled back without falling short of the original requirement?

273. Is the assigned Lean Accounting Best Practices project manager a PMP (Certified Lean Accounting Best Practices project manager) and experienced?

274. Are decisions captured in a decisions log?

275. Is there a formal process for updating the Lean Accounting Best Practices project baseline?

2.11 Activity List: Lean Accounting Best Practices

276. When will the work be performed?

277. How detailed should a Lean Accounting Best Practices project get?

278. Should you include sub-activities?

279. What will be performed?

280. Who will perform the work?

281. When do the individual activities need to start and finish?

282. How much slack is available in the Lean Accounting Best Practices project?

283. Is infrastructure setup part of your Lean Accounting Best Practices project?

284. Are the required resources available or need to be acquired?

285. What is the probability the Lean Accounting Best Practices project can be completed in xx weeks?

286. How do you determine the late start (LS) for each activity?

287. How will it be performed?

288. What is the LF and LS for each activity?

289. What is the total time required to complete the Lean Accounting Best Practices project if no delays occur?

290. What went right?

291. In what sequence?

292. How should ongoing costs be monitored to try to keep the Lean Accounting Best Practices project within budget?

293. How can the Lean Accounting Best Practices project be displayed graphically to better visualize the activities?

294. What did not go as well?

2.12 Activity Attributes: Lean Accounting Best Practices

295. Is there a trend during the year?

296. How many days do you need to complete the work scope with a limit of X number of resources?

297. Were there other ways you could have organized the data to achieve similar results?

298. Have constraints been applied to the start and finish milestones for the phases?

299. Would you consider either of corresponding activities an outlier?

300. How difficult will it be to complete specific activities on this Lean Accounting Best Practices project?

301. How difficult will it be to do specific activities on this Lean Accounting Best Practices project?

302. What is the general pattern here?

303. What is missing?

304. Activity: what is In the Bag?

305. Resource is assigned to?

306. Why?

307. Time for overtime?

308. What activity do you think you should spend the most time on?

309. Activity: what is Missing?

310. Where else does it apply?

311. Has management defined a definite timeframe for the turnaround or Lean Accounting Best Practices project window?

2.13 Milestone List: Lean Accounting Best Practices

312. It is to be a narrative text providing the crucial aspects of your Lean Accounting Best Practices project proposal answering what, who, how, when and where?

313. Usps (unique selling points)?

314. Information and research?

315. What is the market for your technology, product or service?

316. What background experience, skills, and strengths does the team bring to your organization?

317. Can you derive how soon can the whole Lean Accounting Best Practices project finish?

318. Level of the Innovation?

319. Reliability of data, plan predictability?

320. Milestone pages should display the UserID of the person who added the milestone. Does a report or query exist that provides this audit information?

321. How late can the activity finish?

322. How difficult will it be to do specific activities on this Lean Accounting Best Practices project?

323. Describe your organizations strengths and core competencies. What factors will make your organization succeed?

324. What date will the task finish?

325. Sustainable financial backing?

326. Insurmountable weaknesses?

327. Competitive advantages?

328. Identify critical paths (one or more) and which activities are on the critical path?

329. Legislative effects?

330. Environmental effects?

331. Calculate how long can activity be delayed?

2.14 Network Diagram: Lean Accounting Best Practices

332. What are the Major Administrative Issues?

333. What is the completion time?

334. If a current contract exists, can you provide the vendor name, contract start, and contract expiration date?

335. Planning: who, how long, what to do?

336. What controls the start and finish of a job?

337. What are the Key Success Factors?

338. What are the tools?

339. What activity must be completed immediately before this activity can start?

340. What is the probability of completing the Lean Accounting Best Practices project in less that xx days?

341. What is the lowest cost to complete this Lean Accounting Best Practices project in xx weeks?

342. Are you on time?

343. What job or jobs could run concurrently?

344. Can you calculate the confidence level?

345. If x is long, what would be the completion time if you break x into two parallel parts of y weeks and z weeks?

346. How confident can you be in your milestone dates and the delivery date?

347. What activities must occur simultaneously with this activity?

348. What job or jobs precede it?

349. Review the logical flow of the network diagram. Take a look at which activities you have first and then sequence the activities. Do they make sense?

350. How difficult will it be to do specific activities on this Lean Accounting Best Practices project?

351. What must be completed before an activity can be started?

2.15 Activity Resource Requirements: Lean Accounting Best Practices

352. Is there anything planned that does not need to be here?

353. What are constraints that you might find during the Human Resource Planning process?

354. Other support in specific areas?

355. Organizational Applicability?

356. Anything else?

357. What is the Work Plan Standard?

358. Why do you do that?

359. How do you handle petty cash?

360. When does monitoring begin?

361. Which logical relationship does the PDM use most often?

362. Do you use tools like decomposition and rolling-wave planning to produce the activity list and other outputs?

363. Are there unresolved issues that need to be addressed?

364. How many signatures do you require on a check and does this match what is in your policy and procedures?

2.16 Resource Breakdown Structure: Lean Accounting Best Practices

365. What is the difference between % Complete and % work?

366. What defines a successful Lean Accounting Best Practices project?

367. Are the required resources available?

368. Who is allowed to perform which functions?

369. Which resource planning tool provides information on resource responsibility and accountability?

370. Any changes from stakeholders?

371. Why time management?

372. The list could probably go on, but, the thing that you would most like to know is, How long & How much?

373. What is each stakeholders desired outcome for the Lean Accounting Best Practices project?

374. Goals for the Lean Accounting Best Practices project. What is each stakeholders desired outcome for the Lean Accounting Best Practices project?

375. Who will be used as a Lean Accounting Best

Practices project team member?

376. Why do you do it?

377. What are the requirements for resource data?

378. What defines a successful Lean Accounting Best Practices project?

379. When do they need the information?

380. Why is this important?

381. Who will use the system?

382. What is the primary purpose of the human resource plan?

383. Is predictive resource analysis being done?

2.17 Activity Duration Estimates: Lean Accounting Best Practices

384. Which is the BEST thing to do to try to complete a Lean Accounting Best Practices project two days earlier?

385. Why should Lean Accounting Best Practices project managers strive to make jobs look easy?

386. What is the career outlook for Lean Accounting Best Practices project managers in information technology?

387. Will it help in finding or retaining employees?

388. Does a process exist for approving or rejecting changes?

389. How do functionality, system outputs, performance, reliability, and maintainability requirements affect quality planning?

390. What tasks must precede this task?

391. After how many days will the lease cost be the same as the purchase cost for the equipment?

392. Research risk management software. Are many products available?

393. Are contractor costs, schedule and technical performance monitored throughout the Lean

Accounting Best Practices project?

394. What are the advantages and disadvantages of PERT?

395. Which tips for taking the PMP exam do you think would be most helpful for you?

396. Is the Lean Accounting Best Practices project performing better or worse than planned?

397. Which suggestions do you find most useful?

398. What type of contract was used and why?

399. Calculate the expected duration for an activity that has a most likely time of 5, a pessimistic time of 13, and a optimiztic time of 3?

400. Are actual Lean Accounting Best Practices project results compared with planned or expected results to determine the variance?

401. Are expert judgment and historical information utilized to estimate activity duration?

402. Which is a benefit of an analogous Lean Accounting Best Practices project estimate?

2.18 Duration Estimating Worksheet: Lean Accounting Best Practices

403. What info is needed?

404. For other activities, how much delay can be tolerated?

405. Value pocket identification & quantification what are value pockets?

406. How should ongoing costs be monitored to try to keep the Lean Accounting Best Practices project within budget?

407. What questions do you have?

408. What is your role?

409. When does your organization expect to be able to complete it?

410. When, then?

411. Done before proceeding with this activity or what can be done concurrently?

412. Define the work as completely as possible. What work will be included in the Lean Accounting Best Practices project?

413. Is this operation cost effective?

414. How can the Lean Accounting Best Practices project be displayed graphically to better visualize the activities?

415. What is next?

416. Is a construction detail attached (to aid in explanation)?

417. Why estimate costs?

418. Do any colleagues have experience with your organization and/or RFPs?

419. What utility impacts are there?

420. Can the Lean Accounting Best Practices project be constructed as planned?

421. What is an Average Lean Accounting Best Practices project?

2.19 Project Schedule: Lean Accounting Best Practices

422. Did the Lean Accounting Best Practices project come in under budget?

423. Why or why not?

424. Is the structure for tracking the Lean Accounting Best Practices project schedule well defined and assigned to a specific individual?

425. How can you fix it?

426. Master Lean Accounting Best Practices project schedule?

427. Are all remaining durations correct?

428. Why is this particularly bad?

429. Month Lean Accounting Best Practices project take?

430. How can you address that situation?

431. Your best shot for providing estimations how complex/how much work does the activity require?

432. How do you know that youhave done this right?

433. What is the difference?

434. To what degree is do you feel the entire team was committed to the Lean Accounting Best Practices project schedule?

435. How closely did the initial Lean Accounting Best Practices project Schedule compare with the actual schedule?

436. What is Lean Accounting Best Practices project management?

2.20 Cost Management Plan: Lean Accounting Best Practices

437. Environmental management – what changes in statutory environmental compliance requirements are anticipated during the Lean Accounting Best Practices project?

438. Is the structure for tracking the Lean Accounting Best Practices project schedule well defined and assigned to a specific individual?

439. Is your organization certified as a broker of the products/supplies?

440. Was the scope definition used in task sequencing?

441. What is Lean Accounting Best Practices project management?

442. Are the payment terms being followed?

443. Has a structured approach been used to break work effort into manageable components (WBS)?

444. Have Lean Accounting Best Practices project team accountabilities & responsibilities been clearly defined?

445. Have Lean Accounting Best Practices project management standards and procedures been identified / established and documented?

446. Is the Lean Accounting Best Practices project sponsor clearly communicating the business case or rationale for why this Lean Accounting Best Practices project is needed?

447. Is a pmo (Lean Accounting Best Practices project management office) in place and provide oversight to the Lean Accounting Best Practices project?

448. Were Lean Accounting Best Practices project team members involved in detailed estimating and scheduling?

449. Has the budget been baselined?

450. Risk Analysis?

451. Is there a Steering Committee in place?

452. Has a resource management plan been created?

453. Are enough systems & user personnel assigned to the Lean Accounting Best Practices project?

454. Are issues raised, assessed, actioned, and resolved in a timely and efficient manner?

455. Are Lean Accounting Best Practices project contact logs kept up to date?

456. Are vendor invoices audited for accuracy before payment?

2.21 Activity Cost Estimates: Lean Accounting Best Practices

457. What procedures are put in place regarding bidding and cost comparisons, if any?

458. What is the activity recast of the budget?

459. What defines a successful Lean Accounting Best Practices project?

460. Based on your Lean Accounting Best Practices project communication management plan, what worked well?

461. What areas does the group agree are the biggest success on the Lean Accounting Best Practices project?

462. Did the consultant work with local staff to develop local capacity?

463. In which phase of the acquisition process cycle does source qualifications reside?

464. Can you delete activities or make them inactive?

465. What is the last item a Lean Accounting Best Practices project manager must do to finalize Lean Accounting Best Practices project close-out?

466. How do you do activity recasts?

467. Which contract type places the most risk on the seller?

468. What are the audit requirements?

469. How do you fund change orders?

470. Does the activity use a common approach or business function to deliver its results?

471. Scope statement only direct or indirect costs as well?

472. Can you change your activities?

473. What makes a good activity description?

474. Would you hire them again?

475. How do you treat administrative costs in the activity inventory?

2.22 Cost Estimating Worksheet: Lean Accounting Best Practices

476. What is the estimated labor cost today based upon this information?

477. What additional Lean Accounting Best Practices project(s) could be initiated as a result of this Lean Accounting Best Practices project?

478. Identify the timeframe necessary to monitor progress and collect data to determine how the selected measure has changed?

479. How will the results be shared and to whom?

480. Who is best positioned to know and assist in identifying corresponding factors?

481. Will the Lean Accounting Best Practices project collaborate with the local community and leverage resources?

482. Does the Lean Accounting Best Practices project provide innovative ways for stakeholders to overcome obstacles or deliver better outcomes?

483. What happens to any remaining funds not used?

484. Ask: are others positioned to know, are others credible, and will others cooperate?

485. What will others want?

486. Is it feasible to establish a control group arrangement?

487. What costs are to be estimated?

488. What can be included?

489. Can a trend be established from historical performance data on the selected measure and are the criteria for using trend analysis or forecasting methods met?

490. What is the purpose of estimating?

491. Is the Lean Accounting Best Practices project responsive to community need?

2.23 Cost Baseline: Lean Accounting Best Practices

492. Review your risk triggers -have your risks changed?

493. Has the appropriate access to relevant data and analysis capability been granted?

494. Are procedures defined by which the cost baseline may be changed?

495. If you sold 10x widgets on a day, what would the affect on profits be?

496. Does the suggested change request seem to represent a necessary enhancement to the product?

497. Lean Accounting Best Practices project goals -should others be reconsidered?

498. What is your organizations history in doing similar tasks?

499. Has the Lean Accounting Best Practices projected annual cost to operate and maintain the product(s) or service(s) been approved and funded?

500. Is request in line with priorities?

501. Has the Lean Accounting Best Practices project documentation been archived or otherwise disposed as described in the Lean Accounting Best Practices

project communication plan?

502. Who will use corresponding metrics ?

503. Have the resources used by the Lean Accounting Best Practices project been reassigned to other units or Lean Accounting Best Practices projects?

504. Have all approved changes to the schedule baseline been identified and impact on the Lean Accounting Best Practices project documented?

505. What is the consequence?

506. Does the suggested change request represent a desired enhancement to the products functionality?

507. Has the documentation relating to operation and maintenance of the product(s) or service(s) been delivered to, and accepted by, operations management?

508. Have you identified skills that are missing from your team?

509. When should cost estimates be developed?

510. Are there contingencies or conditions related to the acceptance?

2.24 Quality Management Plan: Lean Accounting Best Practices

511. How are your organizations compensation and recognition approaches and the performance management system used to reinforce high performance?

512. Have all stakeholders been identified?

513. How are data handled when a test is not run per specification?

514. Are there standards for code development?

515. Who gets results of work?

516. How do senior leaders create and communicate values and performance expectations?

517. Are you meeting the quality standards?

518. Are requirements management tracking tools and procedures in place?

519. Contradictory information between document sections?

520. How do senior leaders create your organizational focus on customers and other stakeholders?

521. How do you field-modify testing procedures?

522. Where do you focus?

523. Who is responsible?

524. Has a Lean Accounting Best Practices project Communications Plan been developed?

525. Is it necessary?

526. Have Lean Accounting Best Practices project management standards and procedures been established and documented?

527. Does the Lean Accounting Best Practices project have a formal Lean Accounting Best Practices project Plan?

528. Have all necessary approvals been obtained?

529. What procedures are used to determine if you use, and the number of split, replicate or duplicate samples taken at a site?

2.25 Quality Metrics: Lean Accounting Best Practices

530. Do you know how much profit a 10% decrease in waste would generate?

531. Has it met internal or external standards?

532. How exactly do you define when differences exist?

533. What level of statistical confidence do you use?

534. Did evaluation start on time?

535. The metrics–what is being considered?

536. Where is quality now?

537. How should customers provide input?

538. What approved evidence based screening tools can be used?

539. Can you correlate your quality metrics to profitability?

540. Which are the right metrics to use?

541. What documentation is required?

542. Are quality metrics defined?

543. Which data do others need in one place to target areas of improvement?

544. Filter visualizations of interest?

545. What percentage are outcome-based?

546. Has trace of defects been initiated?

547. Are interface issues coordinated?

548. How do you calculate corresponding metrics?

2.26 Process Improvement Plan: Lean Accounting Best Practices

549. Are you following the quality standards?

550. Are you making progress on your improvement plan?

551. What personnel are the coaches for your initiative?

552. What is the test-cycle concept?

553. Where do you want to be?

554. Has a process guide to collect the data been developed?

555. Who should prepare the process improvement action plan?

556. Management commitment at all levels?

557. Everyone agrees on what process improvement is, right?

558. Are you making progress on the goals?

559. Are you making progress on the improvement framework?

560. Does your process ensure quality?

561. What is quality and how will you ensure it?

562. What personnel are the champions for the initiative?

563. To elicit goal statements, do you ask a question such as, What do you want to achieve?

564. The motive is determined by asking, Why do you want to achieve this goal?

565. Have storage and access mechanisms and procedures been determined?

566. Why do you want to achieve the goal?

2.27 Responsibility Assignment Matrix: Lean Accounting Best Practices

567. Is work progressively subdivided into detailed work packages as requirements are defined?

568. What simple tool can you use to help identify and prioritize Lean Accounting Best Practices project risks that is very low tech and high touch?

569. Are too many reports done in writing instead of verbally?

570. Who is the Lean Accounting Best Practices project Manager?

571. Are there any drawbacks to using a responsibility assignment matrix?

572. Are people encouraged to bring up issues?

573. Do work packages consist of discrete tasks which are adequately described?

574. Too many rs: with too many people labeled as doing the work, are there too many hands involved?

575. Does the contractors system include procedures for measuring the performance of critical subcontractors?

576. What is the purpose of assigning and

documenting responsibility?

577. Is data disseminated to the contractors management timely, accurate, and usable?

578. Will too many Communicating responsibilities tangle the Lean Accounting Best Practices project in unnecessary communications?

579. Are meaningful indicators identified for use in measuring the status of cost and schedule performance?

580. Are detailed work packages planned as far in advance as practicable?

581. The anticipated business volume?

582. Are the requirements for all items of overhead established by rational, traceable processes?

583. Identify and isolate causes of favorable and unfavorable cost and schedule variances?

584. What are some important Lean Accounting Best Practices project communications management tools?

585. Do all the identified groups or people really need to be consulted?

2.28 Roles and Responsibilities: Lean Accounting Best Practices

586. Are your policies supportive of a culture of quality data?

587. What is working well?

588. Are your budgets supportive of a culture of quality data?

589. What are your major roles and responsibilities in the area of performance measurement and assessment?

590. Authority: what areas/Lean Accounting Best Practices projects in your work do you have the authority to decide upon and act on the already stated decisions?

591. What expectations were NOT met?

592. Concern: where are you limited or have no authority, where you can not influence?

593. Do you take the time to clearly define roles and responsibilities on Lean Accounting Best Practices project tasks?

594. What specific behaviors did you observe?

595. What is working well within your organizations performance management system?

596. Is feedback clearly communicated and non-judgmental?

597. Attainable / achievable: the goal is attainable; can you actually accomplish the goal?

598. To decide whether to use a quality measurement, ask how will you know when it is achieved?

599. What should you do now to prepare yourself for a promotion, increased responsibilities or a different job?

600. Does the team have access to and ability to use data analysis tools?

601. Have you ever been a part of this team?

602. Accountabilities: what are the roles and responsibilities of individual team members?

603. What areas of supervision are challenging for you?

2.29 Human Resource Management Plan: Lean Accounting Best Practices

604. Who will be impacted (both positively and negatively) as a result of or during the execution of this Lean Accounting Best Practices project?

605. Are parking lot items captured?

606. What is the boss?

607. Are Lean Accounting Best Practices project team members involved in detailed estimating and scheduling?

608. Is quality monitored from the perspective of the customers needs and expectations?

609. Has a quality assurance plan been developed for the Lean Accounting Best Practices project?

610. Are people motivated to meet the current and future challenges?

611. Are meeting minutes captured and sent out after the meeting?

612. Is this Lean Accounting Best Practices project carried out in partnership with other groups/ organizations?

613. Is there a Quality Management Plan?

614. What areas were overlooked on this Lean Accounting Best Practices project?

615. Are estimating assumptions and constraints captured?

616. How relevant is this attribute to this Lean Accounting Best Practices project or audit?

617. Do people have the competencies to meet the strategic objectives?

618. Are all vendor contracts closed out?

619. Is Lean Accounting Best Practices project status reviewed with the steering and executive teams at appropriate intervals?

620. Are Lean Accounting Best Practices project contact logs kept up to date?

621. Account for the purpose of this Lean Accounting Best Practices project by describing, at a high-level, what will be done. What is this Lean Accounting Best Practices project aiming to achieve?

2.30 Communications Management Plan: Lean Accounting Best Practices

622. Do you prepare stakeholder engagement plans?

623. What are the interrelationships?

624. Do you then often overlook a key stakeholder or stakeholder group?

625. What to learn?

626. How often do you engage with stakeholders?

627. How were corresponding initiatives successful?

628. Which stakeholders can influence others?

629. What steps can you take for a positive relationship?

630. Which team member will work with each stakeholder?

631. How do you manage communications?

632. Do you feel a register helps?

633. What approaches do you use?

634. What does the stakeholder need from the team?

635. How did the term stakeholder originate?

636. Are others part of the communications management plan?

637. What approaches to you feel are the best ones to use?

638. Do you have members of your team responsible for certain stakeholders?

639. Who will use or be affected by the result of a Lean Accounting Best Practices project?

640. What is the stakeholders level of authority?

2.31 Risk Management Plan: Lean Accounting Best Practices

641. What risks are necessary to achieve success?

642. Is Lean Accounting Best Practices project scope stable?

643. What are the chances the risk event will occur?

644. What would you do?

645. Are team members trained in the use of the tools?

646. Are you on schedule?

647. Are enough people available?

648. Are end-users enthusiastically committed to the Lean Accounting Best Practices project and the system/product to be built?

649. Technology risk: is the Lean Accounting Best Practices project technically feasible?

650. Maximize short-term return on investment?

651. Why do you need to manage Lean Accounting Best Practices project Risk?

652. Is the process supported by tools?

653. Is the process being followed?

654. How much risk protection can you afford?

655. Have top software and customer managers formally committed to support the Lean Accounting Best Practices project?

656. Was an original risk assessment/risk management plan completed?

657. How well were you able to manage your risk before?

658. What can you do to minimize the impact if it does?

659. Is the necessary data being captured and is it complete and accurate?

660. Methodology: how will risk management be performed on this Lean Accounting Best Practices project?

2.32 Risk Register: Lean Accounting Best Practices

661. What can be done about it?

662. Severity Prediction?

663. Schedule impact/severity estimated range (workdays) assume the event happens, what is the potential impact?

664. What are you going to do to limit the Lean Accounting Best Practices projects risk exposure due to the identified risks?

665. What risks might negatively or positively affect achieving the Lean Accounting Best Practices project objectives?

666. Why would you develop a risk register?

667. Assume the event happens, what is the Most Likely impact?

668. What is a Risk?

669. What may happen or not go according to plan?

670. How are risks graded?

671. Are there any gaps in the evidence?

672. When is it going to be done?

673. Are corrective measures implemented as planned?

674. What is your current and future risk profile?

675. What action, if any, has been taken to respond to the risk?

676. How is a Community Risk Register created?

677. Who is going to do it?

678. Who needs to know about this?

679. What further options might be available for responding to the risk?

2.33 Probability and Impact Assessment: Lean Accounting Best Practices

680. What is the likelihood?

681. How solid is the Lean Accounting Best Practices projection of competitive reaction?

682. Are flexibility and reuse paramount?

683. What is the past performance of the Lean Accounting Best Practices project manager?

684. What would be the effect of slippage?

685. What is the likelihood of a breakthrough?

686. Which of corresponding risk factors can be avoided altogether?

687. Do you have a consistent repeatable process that is actually used?

688. Are requirements fully understood by the software engineering team and customers?

689. Do you manage the process through use of metrics?

690. How well is the risk understood?

691. What are the uncertainties associated with the

technology selected for the Lean Accounting Best Practices project?

692. How do you maximize short-term return on investment?

693. How completely has the customer been identified?

694. Risk categorization -which of your categories has more risk than others?

695. When and how will the recent breakthroughs in basic research lead to commercial products?

696. Are formal technical reviews part of this process?

697. What things are likely to change?

2.34 Probability and Impact Matrix: Lean Accounting Best Practices

698. Does the Lean Accounting Best Practices project team have experience with the technology to be implemented?

699. Could others have been better mitigated?

700. What should be done with risks on the watch list?

701. What are the methods to deal with risks?

702. Amount of reused software?

703. What risks were tracked?

704. What are the ways you measure and evaluate risks?

705. Can it be changed quickly?

706. Economic to take on the Lean Accounting Best Practices project?

707. How would you assess the risk management process in the Lean Accounting Best Practices project?

708. Degree of confidence in estimated size estimate?

709. What are the chances the event will occur?

710. How are the local factors going to affect the

absorption?

711. How do you analyze the risks in the different types of Lean Accounting Best Practices projects?

712. Has something like this been done before?

713. Are staff committed for the duration of the Lean Accounting Best Practices project?

714. To what extent is the chosen technology maturing?

2.35 Risk Data Sheet: Lean Accounting Best Practices

715. What can happen?

716. What will be the consequences if the risk happens?

717. During work activities could hazards exist?

718. Risk of what?

719. Are new hazards created?

720. What is the likelihood of it happening?

721. Do effective diagnostic tests exist?

722. Whom do you serve (customers)?

723. What do people affected think about the need for, and practicality of preventive measures?

724. Potential for recurrence?

725. Type of risk identified?

726. How can it happen?

727. What were the Causes that contributed?

728. What was measured?

729. What is the chance that it will happen?

730. Has the most cost-effective solution been chosen?

731. Has a sensitivity analysis been carried out?

732. What is the environment within which you operate (social trends, economic, community values, broad based participation, national directions etc.)?

733. How reliable is the data source?

2.36 Procurement Management Plan: Lean Accounting Best Practices

734. What is a Lean Accounting Best Practices project Management Plan?

735. Are Lean Accounting Best Practices project leaders committed to this Lean Accounting Best Practices project full time?

736. Is there any form of automated support for Issues Management?

737. Why is procurement planning important?

738. Are updated Lean Accounting Best Practices project time & resource estimates reasonable based on the current Lean Accounting Best Practices project stage?

739. Has the schedule been baselined?

740. Are change requests logged and managed?

741. Are Lean Accounting Best Practices project team roles and responsibilities identified and documented?

742. Are the results of quality assurance reviews provided to affected groups & individuals?

743. Does a documented Lean Accounting Best Practices project organizational policy & plan (i.e. governance model) exist?

744. Have external dependencies been captured in the schedule?

745. Have all documents been archived in a Lean Accounting Best Practices project repository for each release?

746. What were things that you did well, and could improve, and how?

747. Were Lean Accounting Best Practices project team members involved in the development of activity & task decomposition?

748. Is the steering committee active in Lean Accounting Best Practices project oversight?

749. Is the structure for tracking the Lean Accounting Best Practices project schedule well defined and assigned to a specific individual?

750. Has the business need been clearly defined?

2.37 Source Selection Criteria: Lean Accounting Best Practices

751. How do you manage procurement?

752. How should oral presentations be prepared for?

753. If the costs are normalized, please account for how the normalization is conducted. Is a cost realism analysis used?

754. What information is to be provided and when should it be provided?

755. Are they compliant with all technical requirements?

756. When must you conduct a debriefing?

757. In order of importance, which evaluation criteria are the most critical to the determination of your overall rating?

758. Can you identify proposed teaming partners and/or subcontractors and consider the nature and extent of proposed involvement in satisfying the Lean Accounting Best Practices project requirements?

759. What can not be disclosed?

760. Can you reasonably estimate total organization requirements for the coming year?

761. Are evaluators ready to begin this task?

762. Does an evaluation need to include the identification of strengths and weaknesses?

763. Are considerations anticipated?

764. Are resultant proposal revisions allowed?

765. Are types/quantities of material, facilities appropriate?

766. How should oral presentations be evaluated?

767. What are the most critical evaluation criteria that prove to be tiebreakers in the evaluation of proposals?

768. What are the most common types of rating systems?

769. Do you have a plan to document consensus results including disposition of any disagreement by individual evaluators?

2.38 Stakeholder Management Plan: Lean Accounting Best Practices

770. Detail warranty and/or maintenance periods?

771. How are the overall Lean Accounting Best Practices project development processes to be undertaken to produce the Lean Accounting Best Practices project outputs?

772. What is meant by managing the triple constraint?

773. Why would you develop a Lean Accounting Best Practices project Business Plan?

774. Are software metrics formally captured, analyzed and used as a basis for other Lean Accounting Best Practices project estimates?

775. Is it possible to track all classes of Lean Accounting Best Practices project work (e.g. scheduled, un-scheduled, defect repair, etc.)?

776. How are new requirements or changes to requirements identified?

777. How will you engage this stakeholder and gain commitment?

778. Does the resource management plan include a personnel development plan?

779. Have reserves been created to address risks?

780. Is the amount of effort justified by the anticipated value of forming a new process?

781. Are formal code reviews conducted?

782. Have activity relationships and interdependencies within tasks been adequately identified?

783. Has a capability assessment been conducted?

784. Is there an onboarding process in place?

785. Are communication systems currently in place appropriate?

786. What preventative action can be taken to reduce the likelihood a risk will be realised?

787. Who is responsible for arranging and managing the review(s)?

788. Have process improvement efforts been completed before requirements efforts begin?

2.39 Change Management Plan: Lean Accounting Best Practices

789. What is the negative impact of communicating too soon or too late?

790. Has the training provider been established?

791. What would be an estimate of the total cost for the activities required to carry out the change initiative?

792. Who might be able to help you the most?

793. Has the relevant business unit been notified of installation and support requirements?

794. What are the needs, priorities and special interests of the audience?

795. What relationships will change?

796. What is the most cynical response it can receive?

797. Do you need a new organization structure?

798. What risks may occur upfront?

799. Who will be the change levers?

800. How do you know the requirements you documented are the right ones?

801. What work practices will be affected?

802. What are the training strategies?

803. What method and medium would you use to announce a message?

804. What are the major changes to processes?

805. Will the culture embrace or reject this change?

806. What goal(s) do you hope to accomplish?

3.0 Executing Process Group: Lean Accounting Best Practices

807. How does the job market and current state of the economy affect human resource management?

808. Will new hardware or software be required for servers or client machines?

809. What are the typical Lean Accounting Best Practices project management skills?

810. If a risk event occurs, what will you do?

811. How will professionals learn what is expected from them what the deliverables are?

812. How well defined and documented were the Lean Accounting Best Practices project management processes you chose to use?

813. Were sponsors and decision makers available when needed outside regularly scheduled meetings?

814. What good practices or successful experiences or transferable examples have been identified?

815. When do you share the scorecard with managers?

816. How well did the team follow the chosen processes?

817. How can software assist in procuring goods and services?

818. Does the case present a realistic scenario?

819. Do the partners have sufficient financial capacity to keep up the benefits produced by the programme?

820. Does the Lean Accounting Best Practices project team have enough people to execute the Lean Accounting Best Practices project plan?

821. Mitigate. what will you do to minimize the impact should a risk event occur?

822. How well did the chosen processes produce the expected results?

823. What does it mean to take a systems view of a Lean Accounting Best Practices project?

824. What areas were overlooked on this Lean Accounting Best Practices project?

825. What are the main types of goods and services being outsourced?

3.1 Team Member Status Report: Lean Accounting Best Practices

826. How will resource planning be done?

827. Is there evidence that staff is taking a more professional approach toward management of your organizations Lean Accounting Best Practices projects?

828. Does every department have to have a Lean Accounting Best Practices project Manager on staff?

829. Will the staff do training or is that done by a third party?

830. The problem with Reward & Recognition Programs is that the truly deserving people all too often get left out. How can you make it practical?

831. How does this product, good, or service meet the needs of the Lean Accounting Best Practices project and your organization as a whole?

832. Do you have an Enterprise Lean Accounting Best Practices project Management Office (EPMO)?

833. Why is it to be done?

834. What is to be done?

835. Are the products of your organizations Lean Accounting Best Practices projects meeting customers

objectives?

836. Are your organizations Lean Accounting Best Practices projects more successful over time?

837. Does your organization have the means (staff, money, contract, etc.) to produce or to acquire the product, good, or service?

838. Are the attitudes of staff regarding Lean Accounting Best Practices project work improving?

839. How can you make it practical?

840. When a teams productivity and success depend on collaboration and the efficient flow of information, what generally fails them?

841. How much risk is involved?

842. How it is to be done?

843. What specific interest groups do you have in place?

844. Does the product, good, or service already exist within your organization?

3.2 Change Request: Lean Accounting Best Practices

845. How does your organization control changes before and after software is released to a customer?

846. What are the requirements for urgent changes?

847. How many lines of code must be changed to implement the change?

848. How do team members communicate with each other?

849. Who can suggest changes?

850. Should staff call into the helpdesk or go to the website?

851. Who is responsible for the implementation and monitoring of all measures?

852. Does the schedule include Lean Accounting Best Practices project management time and change request analysis time?

853. What are the basic mechanics of the Change Advisory Board (CAB)?

854. Will all change requests and current status be logged?

855. How are changes requested (forms, method of

communication)?

856. What is the change request log?

857. Can you answer what happened, who did it, when did it happen, and what else will be affected?

858. Who is included in the change control team?

859. Who has responsibility for approving and ranking changes?

860. How do you get changes (code) out in a timely manner?

861. Has the change been highlighted and documented in the CSCI?

862. How is quality being addressed on the Lean Accounting Best Practices project?

863. Can static requirements change attributes like the size of the change be used to predict reliability in execution?

864. Who will perform the change?

3.3 Change Log: Lean Accounting Best Practices

865. Is the change backward compatible without limitations?

866. Is the submitted change a new change or a modification of a previously approved change?

867. Is the change request within Lean Accounting Best Practices project scope?

868. Who initiated the change request?

869. Is the change request open, closed or pending?

870. Do the described changes impact on the integrity or security of the system?

871. When was the request approved?

872. How does this change affect the timeline of the schedule?

873. How does this relate to the standards developed for specific business processes?

874. Will the Lean Accounting Best Practices project fail if the change request is not executed?

875. Is this a mandatory replacement?

876. When was the request submitted?

877. Where do changes come from?

878. Should a more thorough impact analysis be conducted?

879. How does this change affect scope?

880. Is the requested change request a result of changes in other Lean Accounting Best Practices project(s)?

3.4 Decision Log: Lean Accounting Best Practices

881. What is the average size of your matters in an applicable measurement?

882. How does provision of information, both in terms of content and presentation, influence acceptance of alternative strategies?

883. How do you know when you are achieving it?

884. Behaviors; what are guidelines that the team has identified that will assist them with getting the most out of team meetings?

885. What are the cost implications?

886. How do you define success?

887. What eDiscovery problem or issue did your organization set out to fix or make better?

888. How does the use a Decision Support System influence the strategies/tactics or costs?

889. Is your opponent open to a non-traditional workflow, or will it likely challenge anything you do?

890. Decision-making process; how will the team make decisions?

891. Do strategies and tactics aimed at less than full

control reduce the costs of management or simply shift the cost burden?

892. With whom was the decision shared or considered?

893. At what point in time does loss become unacceptable?

894. How effective is maintaining the log at facilitating organizational learning?

895. Linked to original objective?

896. Who will be given a copy of this document and where will it be kept?

897. Is everything working as expected?

898. Does anything need to be adjusted?

899. How does an increasing emphasis on cost containment influence the strategies and tactics used?

900. How consolidated and comprehensive a story can you tell by capturing currently available incident data in a central location and through a log of key decisions during an incident?

3.5 Quality Audit: Lean Accounting Best Practices

901. Is there a written corporate quality policy?

902. What review processes are in place for your organizations major activities?

903. How does your organization know that its system for staff performance planning and review is appropriately effective and constructive?

904. How does your organization know that it provides a safe and healthy environment?

905. How does your organization know that its advisory services are appropriately effective and constructive?

906. For each device to be reconditioned, are device specifications, such as appropriate engineering drawings, component specifications and software specifications, maintained?

907. How does your organization know that its support services planning and management systems are appropriately effective and constructive?

908. How does your organization know that its range of activities are being reviewed as rigorously and constructively as they could be?

909. How does your organization know that its system

for recruiting the best staff possible are appropriately effective and constructive?

910. How does your organization know that its staff entrance standards are appropriately effective and constructive and being implemented consistently?

911. How does your organization know that its information technology system is serving its needs as effectively and constructively as is appropriate?

912. Are adequate and conveniently located toilet facilities available for use by the employees?

913. Does the audit organization have experience in performing the required work for entities of your type and size?

914. Is refuse and garbage adequately stored and disposed of with sufficient frequency to prevent contamination?

915. What experience do staff have in the type of work that the audit entails?

916. How does the organization know that its industry and community engagement planning and management systems are appropriately effective and constructive in enabling relationships with key stakeholder groups?

917. What are you trying to do?

918. Are the policies and processes, as set out in the Quality Audit Manual, properly applied?

919. How does your organization know whether they are adhering to mission and achieving objectives?

920. What are your supplier audits?

3.6 Team Directory: Lean Accounting Best Practices

921. Process decisions: which organizational elements and which individuals will be assigned management functions?

922. How will the team handle changes?

923. Does a Lean Accounting Best Practices project team directory list all resources assigned to the Lean Accounting Best Practices project?

924. Who will report Lean Accounting Best Practices project status to all stakeholders?

925. When will you produce deliverables?

926. Where should the information be distributed?

927. Have you decided when to celebrate the Lean Accounting Best Practices projects completion date?

928. Process decisions: do invoice amounts match accepted work in place?

929. How will you accomplish and manage the objectives?

930. Days from the time the issue is identified?

931. Who are your stakeholders (customers, sponsors, end users, team members)?

932. Do purchase specifications and configurations match requirements?

933. Contract requirements complied with?

934. Process decisions: are contractors adequately prosecuting the work?

935. Process decisions: how well was task order work performed?

936. Who will be the stakeholders on your next Lean Accounting Best Practices project?

937. What needs to be communicated?

938. Process decisions: are all start-up, turn over and close out requirements of the contract satisfied?

939. Who will write the meeting minutes and distribute?

3.7 Team Operating Agreement: Lean Accounting Best Practices

940. Why does your organization want to participate in teaming?

941. Reimbursements: how will the team members be reimbursed for expenses and time commitments?

942. What is the anticipated procedure (recruitment, solicitation of volunteers, or assignment) for selecting team members?

943. What administrative supports will be put in place to support the team and the teams supervisor?

944. What is culture?

945. What individual strengths does each team member bring to the group?

946. To whom do you deliver your services?

947. Did you draft the meeting agenda?

948. Do you listen for voice tone and word choice to understand the meaning behind words?

949. Are there more than two functional areas represented by your team?

950. What are the current caseload numbers in the unit?

951. Do you ask participants to close laptops and place mobile devices on silent on the table while the meeting is in progress?

952. Do team members need to frequently communicate as a full group to make timely decisions?

953. What is group supervision?

954. What are the boundaries (organizational or geographic) within which you operate?

955. Do you prevent individuals from dominating the meeting?

956. What resources can be provided for the team in terms of equipment, space, time for training, protected time and space for meetings, and travel allowances?

957. What is the number of cases currently teamed?

958. Are there influences outside the team that may affect performance, and if so, have you identified and addressed them?

959. Are there differences in access to communication and collaboration technology based on team member location?

3.8 Team Performance Assessment: Lean Accounting Best Practices

960. To what degree are the goals realistic?

961. To what degree are the teams goals and objectives clear, simple, and measurable?

962. How do you recognize and praise members for contributions?

963. How do you keep key people outside the group informed about its accomplishments?

964. When a reviewer complains about method variance, what is the essence of the complaint?

965. Social categorization and intergroup behaviour: Does minimal intergroup discrimination make social identity more positive?

966. How hard do you try to make a good selection?

967. To what degree is the team cognizant of small wins to be celebrated along the way?

968. To what degree does the teams work approach provide opportunity for members to engage in results-based evaluation?

969. Can familiarity breed backup?

970. How much interpersonal friction is there in your

team?

971. To what degree are the goals ambitious?

972. To what degree do team members agree with the goals, relative importance, and the ways in which achievement will be measured?

973. Do you promptly inform members about major developments that may affect them?

974. What are teams?

975. To what degree will new and supplemental skills be introduced as the need is recognized?

976. To what degree can all members engage in open and interactive considerations?

977. To what degree can the team ensure that all members are individually and jointly accountable for the teams purpose, goals, approach, and work-products?

978. To what degree can the team measure progress against specific goals?

979. How does Lean Accounting Best Practices project termination impact Lean Accounting Best Practices project team members?

3.9 Team Member Performance Assessment: Lean Accounting Best Practices

980. How accurately is your plan implemented?

981. How are assessments designed, delivered, and otherwise used to maximize training?

982. What happens if a team member receives a Rating of Unsatisfactory?

983. Is there reluctance to join a team?

984. What are the staffs preferences for training on technology-based platforms?

985. Do the goals support your organizations goals?

986. Does the rater (supervisor) have to wait for the interim or final performance assessment review to tell an employee that the employees performance is unsatisfactory?

987. To what degree do team members feel that the purpose of the team is important, if not exciting?

988. Who receives a benchmark visit?

989. What are best practices for delivering and developing training evaluations to maximize the benefits of leveraging emerging technologies?

990. How do you currently account for your results in the teams achievement?

991. What are acceptable governance changes?

992. Verify business objectives. Are they appropriate, and well-articulated?

993. What are best practices in use for the performance measurement system?

994. How should adaptive assessments be implemented?

995. Does platform-specific assessment information contribute to training placement or tailoring of instruction (e.g. aptitude-treatment interaction)?

996. Which training platform formats (i.e., mobile, virtual, videogame-based) were implemented in your effort(s)?

997. To what degree does the team possess adequate membership to achieve its ends?

998. What instructional strategies were developed/ incorporated (e.g., direct instruction, indirect instruction, experiential learning, independent study, interactive instruction)?

999. To what degree are sub-teams possible or necessary?

3.10 Issue Log: Lean Accounting Best Practices

1000. Is the issue log kept in a safe place?

1001. Are there common objectives between the team and the stakeholder?

1002. How much time does it take to do it?

1003. What help do you and your team need from the stakeholders?

1004. How do you manage human resources?

1005. How were past initiatives successful?

1006. Is access to the Issue Log controlled?

1007. Are they needed?

1008. Why do you manage human resources?

1009. In your work, how much time is spent on stakeholder identification?

1010. Are you constantly rushing from meeting to meeting?

1011. What are the stakeholders interrelationships?

1012. What would have to change?

1013. Why not more evaluators?

1014. Who is involved as you identify stakeholders?

1015. What is a Stakeholder?

1016. What steps can you take for positive relationships?

4.0 Monitoring and Controlling Process Group: Lean Accounting Best Practices

1017. What business situation is being addressed?

1018. What were things that you did very well and want to do the same again on the next Lean Accounting Best Practices project?

1019. Just how important is your work to the overall success of the Lean Accounting Best Practices project?

1020. Did it work?

1021. Is the program making progress in helping to achieve the set results?

1022. Is there undesirable impact on staff or resources?

1023. How is agile program management done?

1024. How well did the chosen processes fit the needs of the Lean Accounting Best Practices project?

1025. Do the products created live up to the necessary quality?

1026. What are the goals of the program?

1027. In what way has the program come up with innovative measures for problem-solving?

1028. What is the timeline for the Lean Accounting Best Practices project?

1029. How can you monitor progress?

1030. What factors are contributing to progress or delay in the achievement of products and results?

1031. What are the deliverables?

1032. What resources (both financial and non-financial) are available/needed?

1033. What areas does the group agree are the biggest success on the Lean Accounting Best Practices project?

4.1 Project Performance Report: Lean Accounting Best Practices

1034. How is the data used?

1035. To what degree does the informal organization make use of individual resources and meet individual needs?

1036. To what degree do all members feel responsible for all agreed-upon measures?

1037. What degree are the relative importance and priority of the goals clear to all team members?

1038. To what degree are the demands of the task compatible with and converge with the relationships of the informal organization?

1039. To what degree can team members meet frequently enough to accomplish the teams ends?

1040. To what degree does the teams approach to its work allow for modification and improvement over time?

1041. To what degree will each member have the opportunity to advance his or her professional skills in all three of the above categories while contributing to the accomplishment of the teams purpose and goals?

1042. To what degree do the structures of the formal organization motivate taskrelevant behavior and facilitate task completion?

1043. To what degree can team members frequently and easily communicate with one another?

1044. What is the PRS?

1045. To what degree will team members, individually and collectively, commit time to help themselves and others learn and develop skills?

1046. To what degree is there centralized control of information sharing?

1047. To what degree do the goals specify concrete team work products?

1048. To what degree are the demands of the task compatible with and converge with the mission and functions of the formal organization?

4.2 Variance Analysis: Lean Accounting Best Practices

1049. Is cost and schedule performance measurement done in a consistent, systematic manner?

1050. Are material costs reported within the same period as that in which BCWP is earned for that material?

1051. What was the cause of the increase in costs?

1052. How are material, labor, and overhead variances calculated and recorded?

1053. Are there changes in the direct base to which overhead costs are allocated?

1054. What should management do?

1055. What is the budgeted cost for work scheduled?

1056. Can process improvements lead to unfavorable variances?

1057. What is the performance to date and material commitment?

1058. Are work packages assigned to performing organizations?

1059. At what point should variances be isolated and brought to the attention of the management?

1060. Are records maintained to show how management reserves are used?

1061. How have the setting and use of standards changed over time?

1062. What is the total budget for the Lean Accounting Best Practices project (including estimates for authorized and unpriced work)?

1063. Are the actual costs used for variance analysis reconcilable with data from the accounting system?

1064. Does the accounting system provide a basis for auditing records of direct costs chargeable to the contract?

1065. Did a new competitor enter the market?

4.3 Earned Value Status: Lean Accounting Best Practices

1066. If earned value management (EVM) is so good in determining the true status of a Lean Accounting Best Practices project and Lean Accounting Best Practices project its completion, why is it that hardly any one uses it in information systems related Lean Accounting Best Practices projects?

1067. Earned value can be used in almost any Lean Accounting Best Practices project situation and in almost any Lean Accounting Best Practices project environment. it may be used on large Lean Accounting Best Practices projects, medium sized Lean Accounting Best Practices projects, tiny Lean Accounting Best Practices projects (in cut-down form), complex and simple Lean Accounting Best Practices projects and in any market sector. some people, of course, know all about earned value, they have used it for years - but perhaps not as effectively as they could have?

1068. Where are your problem areas?

1069. Are you hitting your Lean Accounting Best Practices projects targets?

1070. Validation is a process of ensuring that the developed system will actually achieve the stakeholders desired outcomes; Are you building the right product? What do you validate?

1071. Where is evidence-based earned value in your organization reported?

1072. How does this compare with other Lean Accounting Best Practices projects?

1073. What is the unit of forecast value?

1074. When is it going to finish?

1075. How much is it going to cost by the finish?

1076. Verification is a process of ensuring that the developed system satisfies the stakeholders agreements and specifications; Are you building the product right? What do you verify?

4.4 Risk Audit: Lean Accounting Best Practices

1077. What are the outcomes you are looking for?

1078. If applicable; are compilers and code generators available and suitable for the product to be built?

1079. Does the team have the right mix of skills?

1080. Do you have a realistic budget and do you present regular financial reports that identify how you are going against that budget?

1081. Does your auditor understand your business?

1082. Are procedures developed to respond to foreseeable emergencies and communicated to all involved?

1083. What is happening in other jurisdictions? Could that happen here?

1084. What are the legal implications of not identifying a complete universe of business risks?

1085. To what extent are auditors influenced by the business risk assessment in the audit process, and how can auditors create more effective mental models to more fully examine contradictory evidence?

1086. Is there (or should there be) some impact on the

process of setting materiality when the auditor more effectively identifies higher risk areas of the financial statements?

1087. To what extent should analytical procedures be utilized in the risk-assessment process?

1088. Do you have written and signed agreements/contracts in place for each paid staff member?

1089. Has an event time line been developed?

1090. Are contracts reviewed before renewal?

1091. Is Lean Accounting Best Practices project scope stable?

1092. When your organization is entering into a major contract, does it seek legal advice?

1093. Is the technology to be built new to your organization?

1094. Assessing risk with analytical procedures: do systemsthinking tools help auditors focus on diagnostic patterns?

1095. How do you manage risk?

1096. How effective are your risk controls?

4.5 Contractor Status Report: Lean Accounting Best Practices

1097. Describe how often regular updates are made to the proposed solution. Are corresponding regular updates included in the standard maintenance plan?

1098. Are there contractual transfer concerns?

1099. Who can list a Lean Accounting Best Practices project as organization experience, your organization or a previous employee of your organization?

1100. How long have you been using the services?

1101. What is the average response time for answering a support call?

1102. How does the proposed individual meet each requirement?

1103. If applicable; describe your standard schedule for new software version releases. Are new software version releases included in the standard maintenance plan?

1104. What was the actual budget or estimated cost for your organizations services?

1105. What was the budget or estimated cost for your organizations services?

1106. What process manages the contracts?

1107. What are the minimum and optimal bandwidth requirements for the proposed solution?

1108. What was the overall budget or estimated cost?

1109. What was the final actual cost?

1110. How is risk transferred?

4.6 Formal Acceptance: Lean Accounting Best Practices

1111. How does your team plan to obtain formal acceptance on your Lean Accounting Best Practices project?

1112. How well did the team follow the methodology?

1113. Did the Lean Accounting Best Practices project manager and team act in a professional and ethical manner?

1114. What lessons were learned about your Lean Accounting Best Practices project management methodology?

1115. Who would use it?

1116. What can you do better next time?

1117. Was the Lean Accounting Best Practices project goal achieved?

1118. Who supplies data?

1119. What was done right?

1120. Was the client satisfied with the Lean Accounting Best Practices project results?

1121. Do you buy pre-configured systems or build your own configuration?

1122. Have all comments been addressed?

1123. What is the Acceptance Management Process?

1124. Is formal acceptance of the Lean Accounting Best Practices project product documented and distributed?

1125. Does it do what client said it would?

1126. Was the Lean Accounting Best Practices project work done on time, within budget, and according to specification?

1127. What are the requirements against which to test, Who will execute?

1128. Was business value realized?

1129. Do you buy-in installation services?

1130. General estimate of the costs and times to complete the Lean Accounting Best Practices project?

5.0 Closing Process Group: Lean Accounting Best Practices

1131. Will the Lean Accounting Best Practices project deliverable(s) replace a current asset or group of assets?

1132. When will the Lean Accounting Best Practices project be done?

1133. What were the desired outcomes?

1134. Is the Lean Accounting Best Practices project funded?

1135. What level of risk does the proposed budget represent to the Lean Accounting Best Practices project?

1136. Is there a clear cause and effect between the activity and the lesson learned?

1137. Is this a follow-on to a previous Lean Accounting Best Practices project?

1138. Were cost budgets met?

1139. What can you do better next time, and what specific actions can you take to improve?

1140. What were things that you need to improve?

1141. Are there funding or time constraints?

1142. Measurable - are the targets measurable?

1143. What was learned?

1144. Can the lesson learned be replicated?

1145. Is the Lean Accounting Best Practices project funded?

1146. Did the Lean Accounting Best Practices project management methodology work?

1147. What do you need to do?

1148. What went well?

1149. What is an Encumbrance?

1150. Specific - is the objective clear in terms of what, how, when, and where the situation will be changed?

5.1 Procurement Audit: Lean Accounting Best Practices

1151. Are there procedures to ensure that changes to purchase orders will be updated on the computer files?

1152. Do contracts contain regular reviews, targets and quality standards in order to assess suppliers performance?

1153. Do the buyers always select or authorize the source of supply on other than contract purchases?

1154. Are purchase orders pre-numbered?

1155. When corresponding references were made, was a precise description of the performance not otherwise possible and were the already stated references accompanied by the words or equivalent?

1156. Is a log maintained over the use of signature plates?

1157. Budget controls: does your organization maintain an up-to-date (approved) budget for all funded activities, and perform a comparison of that budget with actual expenditures for each budget category?

1158. Do you learn from benchmarking your own practices with international standards?

1159. Are the responsibilities for monitoring the execution and performance of contracts clearly assigned?

1160. Are travel expenditures monitored to determine that they are in line with other employees and reasonable for the area of travel?

1161. Does the procurement function/unit have the ability to apply electronic procurement?

1162. Were results of the award procedures published?

1163. Is there a record maintained of the procedures followed in the opening of tenders together with the reasons for the acceptance or rejection of tenders received?

1164. Are order quantities, deliveries and payment levels under the contract monitored by an appropriate official?

1165. Are there complementary rules to be used and are they applied?

1166. Did your organization decide for an appropriate and admissible procurement procedure?

1167. Is trend analysis performed on expenditures made by key employees and by vendor?

1168. Were any additional works or deliveries admissible, without recourse to a new procurement procedure?

1169. Are there systems for recording and managing stocks (where part of contract)?

1170. Do at least two people have custodial responsibilities for negotiable checks (one checking on the other)?

5.2 Contract Close-Out: Lean Accounting Best Practices

1171. Has each contract been audited to verify acceptance and delivery?

1172. Was the contract complete without requiring numerous changes and revisions?

1173. Was the contract sufficiently clear so as not to result in numerous disputes and misunderstandings?

1174. How is the contracting office notified of the automatic contract close-out?

1175. What happens to the recipient of services?

1176. Change in knowledge?

1177. Have all contracts been completed?

1178. Have all contract records been included in the Lean Accounting Best Practices project archives?

1179. Was the contract type appropriate?

1180. Change in circumstances?

1181. What is capture management?

1182. Change in attitude or behavior?

1183. Parties: who is involved?

1184. Parties: Authorized?

1185. Are the signers the authorized officials?

1186. Why Outsource?

1187. Have all contracts been closed?

1188. Have all acceptance criteria been met prior to final payment to contractors?

1189. How/when used ?

1190. How does it work?

5.3 Project or Phase Close-Out: Lean Accounting Best Practices

1191. What were the goals and objectives of the communications strategy for the Lean Accounting Best Practices project?

1192. What information is each stakeholder group interested in?

1193. Which changes might a stakeholder be required to make as a result of the Lean Accounting Best Practices project?

1194. Does the lesson educate others to improve performance?

1195. What are they?

1196. When and how were information needs best met?

1197. Planned completion date?

1198. What information did each stakeholder need to contribute to the Lean Accounting Best Practices projects success?

1199. Was the user/client satisfied with the end product?

1200. What benefits or impacts does the stakeholder group expect to obtain as a result of the Lean

Accounting Best Practices project?

1201. What stakeholder group needs, expectations, and interests are being met by the Lean Accounting Best Practices project?

1202. Were the outcomes different from the already stated planned?

1203. What is the information level of detail required for each stakeholder?

1204. Were messages directly related to the release strategy or phases of the Lean Accounting Best Practices project?

1205. What is this stakeholder expecting?

1206. What are the informational communication needs for each stakeholder?

5.4 Lessons Learned: Lean Accounting Best Practices

1207. How well were Lean Accounting Best Practices project issues communicated throughout your involvement in the Lean Accounting Best Practices project?

1208. What if anything has been lacking?

1209. How complete and timely were the materials you were provided to decide whether to proceed from one Lean Accounting Best Practices project lifecycle phase to the next?

1210. What was helpful to know when planning the deployment?

1211. Was the control overhead justified?

1212. What is the frequency of group communications?

1213. What are the influence patterns?

1214. How many government and contractor personnel are authorized for the Lean Accounting Best Practices project?

1215. Are there any hidden conflicts of interest?

1216. How effectively and timely was your organizational change impact identified and planned for?

1217. Is the lesson based on actual Lean Accounting Best Practices project experience rather than on independent research?

1218. Was sufficient advance training conducted and/or information provided to enable the already stated affected by the changes to adjust to and accommodate them?

1219. What could be done to improve the process?

1220. How does the budget cycle affect the case?

1221. Was the purpose of the Lean Accounting Best Practices project, the end products and success criteria clearly defined and agreed at the start?

1222. To what extent was the evolution of risks communicated?

1223. Was the Lean Accounting Best Practices project significantly delayed/hampered by outside dependencies (outside to the Lean Accounting Best Practices project, that is)?

1224. Were any objectives unmet?

1225. How useful was the format and content of the Lean Accounting Best Practices project Status Report to you?

Index

ability 36, 90, 196, 259
absorption   208
accept   142
acceptable   49, 88, 145, 239
acceptance   7, 116, 144, 146, 186, 227, 254-255, 259, 261-262
accepted   116, 141, 186, 232
access 2, 8-10, 26, 66, 145, 185, 192, 196, 235, 240
accomplish   8, 83, 120, 127, 196, 218, 232, 244
according   38, 41, 150, 203, 255
account   36, 53, 153, 198, 213, 239
Accounting   1-14, 16-28, 30-43, 45-58, 60-103, 105-146, 148, 150-165, 167-169, 171-181, 183-189, 191, 193-195, 197-203, 205-209, 211-213, 215, 217, 219-227, 229, 232-234, 236-238, 240, 242-244, 246-252, 254-258, 261, 263-266
accounts   158
accrue 142
accuracy   57, 150, 180
accurate   10, 116, 146, 159-160, 194, 202
accurately   238
achievable   116, 196
achieve   8, 61, 77, 83, 118, 121, 163, 192, 198, 201, 239, 242, 248
achieved   18, 76, 81, 110, 118, 128, 132, 196, 254
achieving   203, 227, 231
acquire   222
acquired   161
across 55
action 48, 95, 98, 101, 131, 142, 156, 191, 204, 216
actionable   56, 121
actioned   180
actions 23, 47, 101, 111, 156, 159, 256
active 153, 212
activities   21-22, 25, 36, 80, 92, 100, 114, 131, 142-143, 160-163, 165-166, 168, 175-176, 181-182, 209, 217, 229, 258
activity 3-4, 32, 34, 139, 152, 161-169, 173-175, 177, 181-182, 212, 216, 256
actual 34, 54, 144, 157-158, 174, 178, 247, 252-253, 258, 266
actually   32, 64, 80, 196, 205, 248
adaptive   239
addition   120

additional   38, 43, 66-67, 144, 183, 259
additions   100
address   20, 90, 177, 215
addressed   169, 224, 235, 242, 255
addressing   36, 110
adequate   152, 157, 230, 239
adequately   43, 193, 216, 230, 233
adhering   231
adjust 93-94, 266
adjusted   228
admissible   259
advance   194, 244, 266
advantage   61, 108
advantages   104, 166, 174
adverse   156
advice 251
advisory   223, 229
affect 69, 72, 113, 120, 148, 150, 152, 173, 185, 203, 207, 219,
225-226, 235, 237, 266
affected   137, 200, 209, 211, 218, 224, 266
affecting   12, 61, 139
afford 202
affordable   88
against34, 94, 151, 156, 237, 250, 255
agenda   234
agendas   117, 142
aggregate   55
agreed   266
Agreement   6, 114, 234
agreements   73, 249, 251
agrees 120, 191
aiming 118, 198
alerts   97
aligned   24
alleged   1
alliance   79
allocate   125
allocated   46, 57, 117, 158, 246
allowances   235
allowed   122, 171, 214
allows 10
almost 248
already   111, 195, 222, 258, 264, 266

Although   131
altogether   205
always 10, 258
ambitious   237
amount   23, 160, 207, 216
amounts   232
amplify60, 122
analogous   174
analysis   3, 6, 10-11, 63, 66, 69, 71, 83, 136, 141, 159, 172,
180, 184-185, 196, 210, 213, 223, 226, 246-247, 259
analytical   251
analyze   2, 59, 63, 67, 208
analyzed   97, 142, 215
announce   218
annual 185
another   154, 245
answer 11-12, 16, 28, 44, 59, 75, 92, 104, 224
answered   27, 43, 58, 74, 91, 103, 128
answering   11, 165, 252
anticipate   150
anybody   138
anyone   30, 106, 126
anything   141, 169, 227-228, 265
appear   1
applicable   12, 93, 144, 227, 250, 252
applied   89, 101, 163, 230, 259
appointed   29, 37
approach   76, 84, 104, 108, 137, 179, 182, 221, 236-237, 244
approaches   87, 90, 139, 187, 199-200
approval   42, 125
approvals   159, 188
approved   32, 73, 141, 148, 153, 159, 185-186, 189, 225, 258
approving   148, 173, 224
architect   150
Architects   8
archived   159, 185, 212
archives   261
arising 131
around107, 126
arranging   216
ascertain   156
asking 1, 8, 192
aspects   165

assess   18, 41, 78, 101, 125, 207, 258
assessed   84, 180
assessing   76, 99, 251
Assessment   5-6, 9-10, 21, 195, 202, 205, 216, 236, 238-239, 250
assets   46, 256
assign   19
assigned   140, 154, 160, 163, 177, 179-180, 212, 232, 246,
259
assigning   193
assignment   5, 193, 234
assist   9, 62, 83, 96, 183, 220, 227
assistant   8
associated   160, 205
Assume   203
Assumption   3, 152
assurance   19, 197, 211
attached   176
attainable   40, 196
attempted   30
attempting   101
attend 18
attendance   29
attendant   88
attended   29
attention   12, 105, 246
attitude   261
attitudes   222
attribute   198
attributes   3, 119, 163, 224
audience   217
audited   180, 261
auditing   18, 100, 113, 247
auditor 250-251
auditors   250-251
audits   231
author 1, 144
authority   66, 144, 195, 200
authorize   258
authorized   140, 247, 262, 265
automated   211
automatic   261
available   24, 26, 37, 43, 51, 61, 74, 87, 96, 107, 132, 159,
161, 171, 173, 201, 204, 219, 228, 230, 243, 250

Average   12, 27, 43, 58, 74, 91, 103, 128, 176, 227, 252
avoided   205
background   10, 133, 165
backing   166
backup   236
backward   225
balanced   89
bandwidth   253
barriers 106
baseline   4, 107, 143, 151, 160, 185-186
baselined   180, 211
baselines   38
basics 120
become   109, 111, 119, 148, 228
before 10, 30, 95, 133, 143, 167-168, 175, 180, 202, 208, 216, 223, 251
beginning   2, 15, 27, 43, 58, 74, 91, 103, 129
behavior   244, 261
behaviors   25, 195, 227
behaviour   236
behind 234
belief   11, 16, 28, 44, 59, 75, 92, 104, 118
believable   116
believe 118, 120
benchmark   238
benefit 1, 17, 24, 27, 98, 136, 159, 174
benefits   22, 45, 47, 51, 62, 104, 110, 113, 118-119, 126, 142, 146, 153, 220, 238, 263
better 8, 39, 50, 84, 162, 174, 176, 183, 207, 227, 254, 256
between   132, 138, 148, 152-153, 156, 171, 187, 240, 256
bidders   145
bidding   181
biggest   52, 81, 181, 243
blinding   72
bother 48
bottom   137
bounce   60, 62
boundaries   43, 235
bounds   43
Breakdown   3-4, 154, 171
briefed 37
brings   33
broken 71

broker 179
brought   246
budget   94, 99, 107, 131, 157-158, 162, 175, 177, 180-181,
247, 250, 252-253, 255-256, 258, 266
budgeted   54, 246
budgets   24, 115, 156, 158, 195, 256
building   23, 101, 134, 139, 248-249
burden 228
business   1, 8, 10, 20, 26, 28, 34, 51, 53, 61, 85, 90, 96, 105,
108-111, 113-115, 118, 122, 126, 132, 147, 152, 156, 180, 182, 194,
212, 215, 217, 225, 239, 242, 250, 255
buyers 258
buy-in 109, 255
calculate   166-167, 174, 190
calculated   246
cannot 157
capability   18, 185, 216
capable   8, 37
capacities   117, 139
capacity   18, 23, 78, 138, 181, 220
capital 105
capitalize   65
capture   56, 102, 261
captured   71, 76, 106, 160, 197-198, 202, 212, 215
capturing   228
career 148, 173
carried 64, 197, 210
caseload   234
categories   206, 244
category   33, 258
caused   1, 48
causes 45, 52, 56, 59, 61, 66, 73, 101, 194, 209
celebrate   90, 232
celebrated   236
center 56
central 228
centrally   89
certain 200
certified   160, 179
challenge   8, 227
challenges   128, 131, 197
champions   192
chance   210

chances   201, 207

change   5-6, 16, 26, 30, 52, 57, 61, 63, 65, 73, 76, 79, 81,
100, 121, 134-135, 140, 144-145, 151, 154, 182, 185-186, 206, 211,
217-218, 223-226, 240, 261, 265

changed   23, 30, 81, 101, 115, 143, 147, 183, 185, 207, 223,
247, 257

changes   18, 32, 35, 38, 53, 73, 88, 95, 100, 110, 116, 121,
141-142, 144, 150, 156, 171, 173, 179, 186, 215, 218, 223-226, 232,
239, 246, 258, 261, 263, 266

changing   93, 126, 136

channel   132

channels   147

chargeable   247

charged   49, 157

Charter   2, 38, 41, 133-134, 140

charts 59

cheaper   50

checked   60, 97, 99, 101, 146

checking   260

checklists   9

checks 260

choice 33, 116, 234

choose   11, 89

chosen 208, 210, 219-220, 242

circumvent   26

claimed   1

clarify 111

classes 215

clearly 11, 16, 22, 28, 35, 41, 44, 59, 75, 87, 92, 104, 146, 150,
179-180, 195-196, 212, 259, 266

client   57, 105, 140, 219, 254-255, 263

clients 24, 33

closed 98, 142, 198, 225, 262

closely 10, 178

Close-Out   7, 181, 261, 263

closest 111

Closing 7, 256

coaches   30, 191

cognizant   236

coherent   143

colleague   117

colleagues   106, 113, 176

collect 66, 95, 183, 191

collected   30, 39, 65, 68, 70
collection   69
combine   90
coming   67, 213
command   93
comments   255
commercial   206
commit   245
commitment   110, 137-138, 191, 215, 246
committed   64, 152, 178, 201-202, 208, 211
committee   153, 180, 212
common   134, 182, 214, 240
community   145, 183-184, 204, 210, 230
companies   1, 99
company   8, 50, 61, 105, 107, 109, 116-117, 122, 126
compare   65, 90, 178, 249
compared   121, 174
comparing   87, 157
comparison   11, 258
compatible   225, 244-245
compelling   33
competing   45
competitor   247
compilers   250
complains   236
complaint   236
complete   1, 9, 11, 25, 28, 37, 42, 151, 162-163, 167, 171,
173, 175, 202, 250, 255, 261, 265
completed   12, 29, 32, 35, 41, 133, 143, 151, 161, 167-168,
202, 216, 261
completely   115, 175, 206
completing   121, 154, 167
completion   32, 40, 132, 139, 142, 157, 167-168, 232, 245, 248,
263
complex   8, 128, 153, 177, 248
complexity   25, 69
compliance   23, 45, 54, 56, 67, 153, 179
compliant   213
complied   233
comply   133
component   229
components   152-153, 179
compute   12

computer	258
computing	115
concept	83, 191
concepts	153
concern	44, 79, 195
concerned	20
concerns	20, 24, 111, 252
concise	144
concrete	82, 245
condition	96
conditions	97, 104, 136, 140, 186
conduct	213
conducted	213, 216, 226, 266
confidence	167, 189, 207
confident	168
confirm	11
conflicts	146, 265
conjure	146
connecting	108
consensus	214
consider	21, 26, 163, 213
considered	17, 26, 48, 189, 228
considers	61
consist 193	
consistent	42, 54, 68, 102, 156, 205, 246
constantly	240
constrain	158
Constraint	3, 152, 215
consultant	8, 181
consulted	112, 194
consulting	50
consumers	115
contact	8, 180, 198
contacts	124
contain	21, 73, 98, 258
contained	1
contains	9
content	40, 227, 266
contents	1-2, 9
context	34, 37, 40
continual	96, 98
continuity	53
continuous	71, 89

contract   7, 157, 167, 174, 182, 222, 233, 247, 251, 258-261
contractor   7, 158, 173, 252, 265
contracts   42, 73, 198, 251-252, 258-259, 261-262
contribute   136, 239, 263
control 2, 34, 53, 71, 92-93, 95, 97-98, 100, 102, 132, 136, 144-145,
158, 184, 223-224, 228, 245, 265
controlled   68, 240
controls   21, 61, 64, 77, 80, 85, 93-95, 98, 100-101, 167, 251,
258
convention   110
converge   244-245
conversion   152
convey   1
cooperate   183
Copyright   1
corporate   229
correct 44, 92, 177
correction   156
corrective   47, 101, 156, 159, 204
correlate   189
correspond   9-10
costing 47
counting   117
counts 117
couple 137
course 30, 57, 248
covering   9, 102
coworker   105
craziest   121
create 17, 72, 104, 109, 122, 187, 250
created   60, 70, 101, 131, 135, 139-140, 142, 160, 180, 204,
209, 215, 242
creating   8, 52
creative   17
creativity   76
credible   183
crisis   23
criteria 2, 5, 9-10, 29, 33, 40, 72, 77-78, 83, 99, 114, 118, 130, 132,
144, 146, 148, 184, 213-214, 262, 266
CRITERION   2, 16, 28, 44, 59, 75, 92, 104
critical 39-40, 60, 83, 95, 98, 106, 152, 166, 193, 213-214
criticism   70
cross-sell   113

crucial 64, 136, 165
crystal 12
Cultural   136
culture 35, 61, 195, 218, 234
current 37, 44, 53, 65, 73, 81, 85, 99, 110, 118, 124-125, 143, 153, 158, 167, 197, 204, 211, 219, 223, 234, 256
currently   41, 109, 216, 228, 235, 239
custodial   260
customer   21, 30-31, 38-39, 77, 99, 102, 107-108, 117, 123, 150, 202, 206, 223
customers   1, 17, 32-33, 48, 55-56, 65, 73, 93, 105, 109-111, 115-116, 120-121, 124, 126, 147, 187, 189, 197, 205, 209, 221, 232
cut-down   248
cycles 134
cynical 217
damage   1
Dashboard   9
dashboards   100
day-to-day   96, 108
deadlines   26, 112, 160
dealing   17
debriefing   213
deceitful   105
decide 80, 195-196, 259, 265
decided   89, 232
deciding   117
decision   6, 47, 72, 75-76, 83-84, 86, 219, 227-228
decisions   75, 82-83, 85-86, 89-90, 94, 100, 103, 132, 136, 160, 195, 227-228, 232-233, 235
decrease   189
dedicated   8
deeper   11
detect 215
defects   190
define 2, 28, 31, 35, 40, 62, 90, 134, 145, 154, 175, 189, 195, 227
defined   11-12, 16, 20-21, 28-29, 31, 35, 38-39, 41-42, 44, 59, 68, 75, 92, 104, 139, 150-151, 153-154, 164, 177, 179, 185, 189, 193, 212, 219, 266
defines 25, 35, 41, 171-172, 181
defining   8, 114
definite   98, 164
definition   22, 25, 30, 36, 38, 43, 179
degree   178, 207, 236-239, 244-245

delayed   166, 266
delaying   48
delays 56, 162
delegated   37
delete 181
deletions   100
deliver 17, 40, 77, 110, 116, 182-183, 234
delivered   49, 118, 144, 186, 238
deliveries   259
delivering   238
delivery   22, 50, 104, 110, 168, 261
demand   128
demands   244-245
department   8, 122, 142, 221
depend   222
dependent   110, 133, 136
depends   105
deploy 98, 119
deployed   97
deploying   50
deployment   265
derive 99, 165
Describe   20, 144, 148, 166, 252
described   1, 156, 185, 193, 225
describing   32, 198
deserving   221
design 1, 10, 70, 78, 80, 93, 108, 144, 153
designated   159
designed   8, 10, 66, 76, 88, 238
designing   8
desired25, 43, 71, 87, 171, 186, 248, 256
detail   78, 134, 155, 176, 215, 264
detailed   60, 63, 131, 158, 161, 180, 193-194, 197
detect 97
determine   10, 112-113, 139, 161, 174, 183, 188, 259
determined   62, 113, 192
detracting   106
develop   52, 75-76, 78, 82, 154, 181, 203, 215, 245
developed   10, 29, 38-39, 83, 143, 145, 186, 188, 191, 197,
225, 239, 248-251
developers   144
developing   62, 85, 156, 238
device 229

devices 235
diagnostic 209, 251
diagram 4, 45, 47, 61, 140, 167-168
Diagrams 48, 153
Dictionary 3, 156
difference 138, 171, 177
different 8, 19, 32-33, 36, 38, 61-62, 113, 115, 138-140, 152-153, 196, 208, 264
difficult 64, 163, 165, 168
dilemma 124
dimensions 22
direct 156, 182, 239, 246-247
direction 30, 50
directions 210
directly 1, 65, 73, 131, 136, 264
Directory 6, 232
Disagree 11, 16, 28, 44, 59, 75, 92, 104
disaster 53
disclosed 213
disclosure 99
discrete 193
discussion 106
display 165
displayed 39, 66, 162, 176
disposed 185, 230
disputes 261
disqualify 64
disruptive 61
distribute 233
Divided 27, 37, 43, 57, 74, 91, 103, 128
document 10, 144, 146-147, 152, 187, 214, 228
documented 35, 87, 89, 94, 96-97, 99, 139, 150, 152-153, 179, 186, 188, 211, 217, 219, 224, 255
documents 8, 152, 159, 212
dominating 235
dormant 124
drawbacks 193
drawings 229
Driver 67
drivers 51
drives 57
driving 125, 127
dropped 160

duplicate   188
duration   4, 155, 157, 173-175, 208
durations   34, 177
during 30, 81, 131, 163, 169, 179, 197, 209, 228
dynamics   34
earlier 122, 173
earned   6, 246, 248-249
easily 245
economic   207, 210
economical   123
economy   90, 219
eDiscovery   227
edition 9
editorial   1
educate   263
education   23, 99
effect 205, 256
effective   18, 20, 118, 125, 127, 146, 152, 156, 175, 209, 228-
230, 250-251
effects 55, 136, 166
efficiency   66, 96
efficient   50, 84, 180, 222
effort   34, 47, 55, 116, 157-158, 179, 216, 239
efforts 30, 78, 143, 216
either   163
electronic   1, 259
element   157-158
elements   10, 28, 67, 102, 113, 143, 156-157, 232
elicit   192
e-mail 147
embarking   33
embrace   218
emerging   64, 99, 238
emphasis   228
employee   80, 113, 238, 252
employees   22, 25-26, 68, 106, 111, 173, 230, 238, 259
employers   135
empower   8
enable 61, 266
enabling   230
encourage   76, 102
encouraged   193
end-users   201

engage 120, 199, 215, 236-237
engagement 56, 135, 199, 230
enhance 97
enhancing 93
enough 8, 73, 105, 115, 127, 144, 146, 148, 180, 201, 220, 244
ensure 34, 67, 70, 88, 105, 107, 116, 118, 144, 152-153, 191-192, 237, 258
ensures 107
ensuring 10, 117, 248-249
entail 45
entails 230
entering 251
Enterprise 54, 221
entire 178
entities 49, 230
entity 1
entrance 230
equipment 22, 25, 131, 173, 235
equipped 37
equitably 37
equivalent 258
errors 122, 156
essence 236
essential 90
essentials 122
establish 75, 98, 184
estimate 48-49, 151, 174, 176, 207, 213, 217, 255
estimated 32, 40, 48, 53, 126, 183-184, 203, 207, 252-253
estimates 4, 33, 44, 69, 143, 157, 173, 181, 186, 211, 215, 247
estimating 4, 175, 180, 183-184, 197-198
estimation 82
etcetera 104
ethical 22, 116, 254
ethnic 122
evaluate 78, 82, 207
evaluated 214
evaluating 77, 83
evaluation 72, 88, 102, 157, 189, 213-214, 236
evaluators 214, 241
events 18, 77, 80, 82
everyday 68

everyone   35, 37, 191
everything   228
evidence   11, 56, 189, 203, 221, 250
evolution   44, 266
evolve 103
exactly 189
examine   250
examined   29
example   2, 9, 13, 22, 60, 96, 152
examples   8-9, 219
exceed   155
exceeding   56
excellence   8, 30
excellent   52
except 156
excess 158
exciting   238
execute   220, 255
executed   225
Executing   6, 219
execution   98, 131, 153, 197, 224, 259
executive   8, 123, 198
executives   106
exercise   20
existing 10, 96, 120, 140, 150
exists   167
expect 127, 175, 263
expected   22, 34, 79, 116, 127, 174, 219-220, 228
expecting   264
expend   47
expense   158
expenses   234
experience   40, 108, 111, 141, 165, 176, 207, 230, 252, 266
experiment   111
expert 174
expertise   90
experts 36
expiration   167
explained   10
explicitly   124
explore   61
exposure   203
exposures   79

extent 11, 20, 24-25, 29, 85, 138, 208, 213, 250-251, 266
external   30, 109, 189, 212
facilitate   11, 22, 59, 100, 245
facilities   147, 214, 230
facing 26, 124
factors 55, 84, 106, 153, 166-167, 183, 205, 207, 243
failure 47, 111, 123
fairly   37
falling 160
familiar9
fashion 1
favorable   194
feasible   49, 61, 124, 184, 201
feature 10
features   141
feedback   30-31, 196
Filter   190
finalize 181
finalized   13
financial   52, 62, 66, 69, 108, 116, 166, 220, 243, 250-251
finding 173
fingertips   10
finish   161, 163, 165-167, 249
finished   143
follow 96, 109, 114, 219, 254
followed   37, 157, 179, 202, 259
following   9, 11, 191
follow-on   256
for--and   94
forecast   249
forefront   117
foreseen   131
forever 115
forget 10
formal 7, 128, 143, 160, 188, 206, 216, 244-245, 254-255
formally   31, 202, 215
format 10, 150, 266
formats   239
forming   216
formula   12
Formulate   28
forward   113, 128
foster   112, 119

framework 93, 126, 191
freaky 115
frequency 29, 100, 113, 230, 265
frequent 159
frequently 49, 51, 235, 244-245
friction 236
friend 117, 124
frontiers 76
fulfill 125
full-blown 51
full-scale 78
function 151, 182, 259
functional 156, 234
functions 31, 71-72, 107, 115, 147, 171, 232, 245
funded 185, 256-258
funding 126-127, 256
further 204
future 8, 55, 77, 102, 106, 136, 140, 158, 197, 204
gained 67, 95, 100
garbage 230
gather 11, 29, 33-34, 36-37, 41-42, 44, 63, 67-68
gathered 42, 61, 64, 66, 68, 71
gathering 29, 41-42, 147
general 84, 152, 163, 255
generally 222
generate 66, 73, 189
generated 63
generation 9, 63
generators 250
geographic 235
getting 50, 227
global 90, 115
govern 125
governance 21, 120, 153, 211, 239
government 157, 265
graded 203
granted 185
graphics 19
graphs 9
greatest 76
ground 62
groups 113, 152-153, 194, 197, 211, 222, 230
growth 72, 106

guarantee   75
guidance   1
guidelines   227
hampered   266
handle 169, 232
handled   187
happen   26, 119, 203, 209-210, 224, 250
happened   224
happening   115, 209, 250
happens   8, 38, 45, 54, 113, 125, 127, 146, 159-160, 183, 203, 209, 238, 261
hardest   48
hardly   248
hardware   219
havent 109
hazards   209
health   119
healthy   229
hearing   122
helpdesk   223
helpful 174, 265
helping   8, 134, 242
hidden 55, 265
higher   157, 251
highest 26
high-level   35, 41, 147, 198
Highly   60
high-tech   119
hiring   99
historical   174, 184
history   143, 185
hitters   60
hitting   248
honest 116
horizon 111
humans   8
hypotheses   59
identified   1, 16, 19, 31, 38, 59, 63, 81, 85, 131, 142-143, 146, 151, 179, 186-187, 194, 203, 206, 209, 211, 215-216, 219, 227, 232, 235, 265
identifies   251
identify 10-11, 20, 26, 60, 64, 79, 156, 160, 166, 183, 193-194, 213, 241, 250

identity 236
ignore 19
ignoring   106
images 146
imbedded   95
impact 5, 36, 44, 49, 51-55, 84, 113, 147, 186, 202-203, 205, 207,
217, 220, 225-226, 237, 242, 250, 265
impacted   45, 150, 153, 197
impacts   48, 52, 153, 176, 263
implement   23, 47, 70, 92, 144, 223
implicit 105
importance   213, 237, 244
important   19, 21, 42, 65, 69, 73, 105, 114, 122, 125, 128, 133,
136, 139, 172, 194, 211, 238, 242
improve   2, 10, 62, 75-77, 79-81, 86, 88, 90, 133, 212, 256,
263, 266
improved   80-81, 85, 87, 98
improving   80, 222
inactive   181
incentives   100
incident   228
include   26, 90, 161, 193, 214-215, 223
included   2, 8, 22, 153, 157, 175, 184, 224, 252, 261
INCLUDES   10
including   18, 30, 35, 41, 50, 52, 66, 95, 101-102, 152, 214,
247
increase   85, 116, 153, 246
increased   106, 196
increasing   127, 228
incurred   55
Incurrence   158
incurring   157
in-depth   9, 11
indicate   64, 96, 118
indicated   101
indicators   16, 50, 56, 65, 68, 71, 73, 85, 101, 157, 194
indirect   49, 156-158, 182, 239
indirectly   1
individual   1, 54, 161, 177, 179, 196, 212, 214, 234, 244, 252
industry   101, 117, 121, 136, 159, 230
infinite 115
influence   76, 122, 135, 195, 199, 227-228, 265
influenced   250

influences 235
inform 237
informal 244
informed 124, 137, 236
ingrained 103
inherent 125
in-house 134
initial 29, 117, 134, 178
initially 43, 144, 158
initiate 156
initiated 183, 190, 225
Initiating 2, 116, 131
initiative 11, 191-192, 217
Innovate 75
innovation 56, 66, 72, 90, 102, 108, 112, 165
innovative 104, 183, 242
in-process 71
inputs 32, 36, 48, 61, 97
inside 19
insight 66, 74
insights 9
inspired 126
instead 124, 193
instructed 144
insure 113
integrate 78, 95, 109
integrity 26, 225
intended 1, 83
INTENT 16, 28, 44, 59, 75, 92, 104
intention 1
intents 138
interact 107
interest 112, 190, 222, 265
interested 263
interests 23, 217, 264
interface 190
interfaces 152
intergroup 236
interim 112, 238
internal 1, 30, 70, 109, 122, 153, 189
interpret 11
intervals 198
interview 110

introduced   150, 237
inventory   182
investment   20, 56, 64, 201, 206
invitee 142
invoice232
invoices   180
involve 108
involved   17, 22, 35, 54, 67-68, 71, 85, 137, 152-153, 180,
193, 197, 212, 222, 241, 250, 261
involves   99
isolate 194
isolated   246
issues   17, 19-20, 23-24, 136, 150, 167, 169, 180, 190, 193, 211,
265
iterative   147
itself   1, 20
joining 150
jointly   237
judgment   1, 174
justified102, 216, 265
killer   104
knowledge   10, 30-31, 40, 67, 81, 90, 95, 97-98, 100-101, 108,
119, 123, 126, 261
labeled   193
lacked 101
lacking265
laptops   235
largely 73
latest   9
leader 18, 60-61, 85
leaders35, 61-62, 108, 119, 187, 211
leadership   20, 35, 40, 90, 119, 137-138
learned   7, 102, 106, 254, 256-257, 265
learning   97-98, 102, 156, 228, 239
lesson 256-257, 263, 266
lessons 7, 78, 102, 106, 254, 265
letter   147
levels   18, 26, 42, 65, 73, 85, 101-102, 119, 154, 191, 259
leverage   30, 90, 102, 111, 183
leveraged   30
leveraging   238
levers   217
liability 1

licensed 1
lifecycle 48, 63, 265
lifecycles 90
lifestyle 136
Lifetime 10
likelihood 82, 86, 205, 209, 216
likely 80, 99, 117, 174, 203, 206, 227
limited 10, 157, 195
linear 147
Linked 31, 228
listed 1
listen 112, 121, 234
locally 89
located 230
location 228, 235
logged 211, 223
logical 168-169
longer 93
long-term 98, 117, 124
looking 24, 250
losing 48
losses 18, 32
lowest 167
machines 219
magnitude 89
maintain 92, 106, 185, 258
maintained 84, 229, 247, 258-259
makers 84, 219
making 18, 72, 76, 86, 107, 191, 242
manage 32-33, 47, 50, 53, 62, 70, 77-78, 84, 87, 89, 104,
126, 131, 133, 140-141, 148, 199, 201-202, 205, 213, 232, 240, 251
manageable 31, 86, 179
managed 8, 38, 63, 69, 75, 80, 85, 88, 96, 100, 150, 211
management 1, 3-5, 9-10, 20-21, 27, 30, 41, 52, 54, 63, 65, 67,
72, 76, 78, 81, 83, 85, 89, 111, 122, 126, 128, 131, 136, 139-144,
150, 152, 156, 159, 164, 171, 173, 178-181, 186-188, 191, 194-195,
197, 199-202, 207, 211, 215, 217, 219, 221, 223, 228-230, 232, 242,
246-248, 254-255, 257, 261
manager 8, 10, 24, 32, 34, 123, 131, 133, 160, 181, 193, 205,
221, 254
managers 2, 130, 156, 173, 202, 219
manages 77, 83, 252
managing 2, 89, 130, 132, 135, 215-216, 260

mandate   133
mandatory   225
manner   18, 90, 132, 152, 156, 180, 224, 246, 254
mantle 121
Manual   230
Mapping   63, 68
marked   151
market 16, 165, 219, 247-248
marketer   8
marketing   115, 147
markets   25
Master 177
material   214, 246
materials   1, 265
matrices   148
Matrix 3, 5, 136, 148, 193, 207
matter 36, 50, 56
matters   227
maturing   208
maximize   201, 206, 238
maximizing   110
meaning   234
meaningful   47, 108, 157, 194
measurable   39-40, 236, 257
measure   2, 10, 18, 21, 30, 37, 44-46, 48, 50-51, 53-54, 57,
66-67, 75, 78, 86-87, 93, 96-97, 101, 103, 151, 183-184, 207, 237
measured   23, 45, 47, 49, 55-56, 87, 94, 97, 209, 237
measures   50-52, 55-56, 65-66, 71, 73, 85, 96, 101, 204, 209,
223, 242, 244
measuring   92, 193-194
mechanical   1
mechanics   223
mechanisms   151, 192
mechanized   159
medium   218, 248
meeting   41-42, 99, 142, 187, 197, 221, 233-235, 240
meetings   29, 36, 42, 142, 145, 219, 227, 235
megatrends   105
member   6, 35, 115, 119, 172, 199, 221, 234-235, 238, 244,
251
members   30, 37, 67, 96, 142, 150, 180, 196-197, 200-201,
212, 223, 232, 234-238, 244-245
membership   239

mental 250
Mentally   144
merely 137
message   100, 218
messages   264
method   46, 141, 218, 223, 236
methods   29, 31, 49, 68, 157, 184, 207
metrics 4, 29, 69, 100, 186, 189-190, 205, 215
Milestone   4, 165, 168
milestones   41, 135, 157, 163
minimal   236
minimize   157, 202, 220
minimizing   62, 110
minimum   253
minority   23
minutes   41, 83, 197, 233
missed 46, 122
missing 66, 125, 163-164, 186
mission 61, 69, 123, 125, 231, 245
Mitigate   82, 220
mitigated   207
mitigation   141, 143
mobile 235, 239
modeling   73
models 16, 74, 109, 250
modified   98
moment   127
moments   64
momentum   108, 122
monetary   27
monitor   97, 100-101, 103, 183, 243
monitored   96-97, 100, 131, 162, 173, 175, 197, 259
monitoring   6, 92-94, 96-97, 102, 150, 169, 223, 242, 259
months 81, 83
Morale 137
motivate   112, 244
motivated   197
motivation   22, 98, 133
motive 192
moving   113
narrative   165
narrow 66
national   210

nature 213
nearest   12
nearly 120
necessary   64, 69, 71, 74, 79, 104, 109, 121, 139, 183, 185,
188, 201-202, 239, 242
needed   17, 22-24, 36, 61, 69-70, 95, 175, 180, 219, 240,
243
negative   115, 217
negatively   197, 203
negotiable   260
negotiate   105
negotiated   114
neither 1
nervous   144
Network   4, 167-168
Neutral 11, 16, 28, 44, 59, 75, 92, 104
normal 103, 156
normalized   213
notice 1, 138
notified   217, 261
number   27, 43, 51, 57, 74, 91, 103, 128, 163, 188, 235, 267
numbers   120, 234
numerous   261
objection   17-18
objective   8, 57, 136, 157, 228, 257
objectives   18, 21, 24, 28, 31, 39, 61, 69, 95, 99, 105, 116, 118,
127, 132, 138, 142, 153, 198, 203, 222, 231-232, 236, 239-240, 263,
266
observe   195
observed   90
observing   153
obsolete   105
obstacles   26, 183
obtain 121, 254, 263
obtained   30, 188
obtaining   48
obviously   11
occurring   82, 131
occurs 23, 53, 95, 219
offerings   65, 90
office   180, 221, 261
official 259
officials 262

onboarding   216
one-time   8
ongoing   76, 97, 162, 175
opening   259
operate   185, 210, 235
operates   117
operating   6, 49, 56, 102, 139, 234
operation   94, 175, 186
operations   10, 93, 95, 99, 103, 186
operators   96
opponent   227
opposite   117-118
opposition   127
optimal   89, 253
optimize   76, 92
optimized   113
optimiztic   174
option 116
options24, 204
orders 182, 258
organize   141
organized   163
orient 99
origin   146
original160, 202, 228
originally   153
originate   199
others   132, 183, 185, 190, 199-200, 206-207, 245, 263
otherwise   1, 185, 238, 258
outcome   11, 75, 171
outcomes   77, 82, 93, 108, 183, 248, 250, 256, 264
outlier 163
outlined   99
outlook   173
output 30, 59-60, 65-66, 69-72, 96-97
outputs   32, 61, 68-70, 72-73, 97, 151, 169, 173, 215
outside76, 131, 219, 235-236, 266
Outsource   62, 262
outsourced   220
outweigh   47
overall 11, 24, 53, 95, 113, 119, 153, 213, 215, 242, 253
overcome   183
overhead   194, 246, 265

overlook 199
overlooked 198, 220
oversight 71, 153, 180, 212
overtime 164
owners 154
ownership 41, 101
package 156
packages 157, 193-194, 246
paradigms 118
paragraph 106
parallel 168
parameters 98
paramount 205
Pareto 59
parking 197
particular 60
Parties 79, 142, 261-262
partners 17, 35, 79, 105, 111, 119, 139, 213, 220
pattern 163
patterns 78, 251, 265
paycheck 126
paying 105
payment 159, 179-180, 259, 262
pending 225
people 8, 19, 52-53, 62, 70, 85, 87, 95, 102, 104-105, 107, 111-112, 117, 120-121, 124-125, 193-194, 197-198, 201, 209, 220-221, 236, 248, 260
perceive 117
percent 122
percentage 148, 190
perception 77, 87, 116
perform 19, 36-37, 152, 161, 171, 224, 258
performed 76, 148, 161, 202, 233, 259
performing 174, 230, 246
perhaps 23, 248
period 88, 246
periodic 142
periods 215
permission 1
person 1, 24, 142, 165
personal 122
personally 148
personnel 26-27, 64, 97, 180, 191-192, 215, 265

pertinent   97
phased   156
phases 48, 81, 145, 163, 264
Philosophy   137
phrase 144
pitfalls 125
placement   239
places 182
planet 95
planned   94, 96, 98-99, 132, 144, 157, 169, 174, 176, 194,
204, 263-265
planning   3, 9, 95-96, 138, 145, 158, 167, 169, 171, 173, 211,
221, 229-230, 265
plates 258
platform   239
platforms   238
please 213
pocket 175
pockets   175
points 27, 43, 57, 70, 74, 91, 103, 128, 165
policies   195, 230
policy 39, 86, 153, 170, 211, 229
political   37
portfolio   115
portray 59
positioned   183
positive   81, 115, 122, 199, 236, 241
positively   197, 203
possess 239
possible   47, 66, 73, 82, 92, 115-116, 175, 215, 230, 239, 258
potential   17, 55, 64, 82-83, 85, 105, 120, 156, 203, 209
practical   61, 75, 87, 92, 221-222
Practices   1-7, 9-14, 16-28, 30-43, 45-58, 60-103, 105-146,
148, 150-165, 167-169, 171-181, 183-189, 191, 193-195, 197-203,
205-209, 211-213, 215, 217-227, 229, 232-234, 236-240, 242-244,
246-252, 254-258, 261, 263-266
praise 236
precaution   1
precede   168, 173
precise 258
predict 224
predicting   92, 136
Prediction   203

predictive   172
pre-filled   9
prepare   191, 196, 199
prepared   132, 213
present   102, 106, 121, 220, 250
presented   23
preserve   29
preserved   73
prevent   47, 230, 235
preventive   209
prevents   18
previous   30, 131, 252, 256
previously   140, 225
primary   46, 133, 172
priorities   45-46, 52, 55, 57, 185, 217
prioritize   193
priority 50, 53, 244
privacy   32
probably   171
problem   16-17, 19, 22-25, 28-30, 40-41, 46, 50, 61, 67, 137,
145, 221, 227, 248
problems   19-21, 26, 76, 82, 101, 127
procedure   234, 259
procedures   10, 89, 96-97, 99, 102, 157, 170, 179, 181, 185,
187-188, 192-193, 250-251, 258-259
proceed   265
proceeding   175
process   1-4, 6-8, 10, 30, 32, 35-37, 39, 41, 59-74, 80, 90,
96-103, 131, 137-138, 143-144, 147-153, 157, 160, 169, 173, 181,
191, 201-202, 205-207, 216, 219, 227, 232-233, 242, 246, 248-252,
255-256, 266
processes   53, 61-62, 65-72, 96, 99, 102, 137, 139, 153, 194,
215, 218-220, 225, 229-230, 242
procuring   220
produce   66, 169, 215, 220, 222, 232
produced   69, 81, 220
producing   148
product   1, 48, 65, 73, 104, 127, 150-151, 165, 185-186, 201,
221-222, 248-250, 255, 263
production   40, 76, 106, 132
products   1, 20, 22, 52, 105, 107, 136, 138-139, 144, 148,
157, 173, 179, 186, 206, 221, 242-243, 245, 266
profile 204

profit   189
profits   185
program   23, 49, 72, 94, 242
programme   220
Programs   221
progress   37, 49, 78, 95, 107-108, 142, 151, 183, 191, 235, 237, 242-243
prohibited   156
project 2-4, 6-9, 19-20, 29, 51, 62-63, 72, 89, 93, 96, 99, 108, 110, 115, 119, 123, 126, 128, 130-145, 148, 150-157, 159-165, 167-168, 171-181, 183-186, 188, 193-195, 197-198, 200-203, 205-208, 211-213, 215, 219-226, 232-233, 237, 242-244, 247-248, 251-252, 254-257, 261, 263-266
projected   156, 185
projection   205
projects   2, 52, 122, 130, 132-133, 138-139, 148, 150, 154, 186, 195, 203, 208, 221-222, 232, 248-249, 263
promising   104
promote   52, 70
promotion   196
promptly   237
proofing   90
proper 99, 159
properly   35, 39, 131, 230
proposal   165, 214
proposals   214
proposed   23, 53, 76, 82, 140-141, 213, 252-253, 256
protect   64, 108
protected   73, 235
protection   110, 202
provide   23, 74, 118, 123, 125, 135, 138, 144, 147, 157, 167, 180, 183, 189, 236, 247
provided   12, 96, 152, 159, 211, 213, 235, 265-266
provider   217
providers   79
provides   165, 171, 229
providing   99, 135, 165, 177
provision   142, 227
published   259
publisher   1
pulled 122
purchase   8, 173, 233, 258
purchases   258

purpose   2, 10, 122, 132, 172, 184, 193, 198, 237-238, 244, 266
purposes   140
pushing   115
qualified   37, 60, 65, 67, 69-70, 142
qualifies   66, 72
qualify 52, 60, 64
qualities   24
quality 1, 4, 6, 10, 19, 46, 52, 55, 60, 63, 69, 71, 78, 92, 101, 111, 132, 139, 173, 187, 189, 191-192, 195-197, 211, 224, 229-230, 242, 258
quantified   93
quantify   52
quantities   214, 259
question   11-12, 16, 28, 44, 59, 75, 92, 104, 126, 138, 192
questions   8-9, 11, 61, 175
quickly 10, 60, 62, 207
radically   61
raised 180
ranking224
rather 124, 266
rating 213-214, 238
rational   156, 194
rationale   180
reached   23
reaching   106, 127
reaction   205
reactivate   124
readiness   40
readings   101
realised   216
realism 213
realistic   23, 67, 111, 220, 236, 250
realize 49
realized   126, 255
really   8, 19, 29, 194
reason 118, 126
reasonable   86, 128, 140, 143, 159, 211, 259
reasonably   157, 213
reasons   33, 142, 156, 259
reassess   142
reassigned   186
rebuild 104

recast 181
recasts 181
receive   9-10, 32, 48, 217
received   37, 119, 259
receives   238
recent 206
recently   123
recipient   24, 261
recognised   80
recognize   2, 16-21, 23, 27, 78, 85, 90, 236
recognized   17-19, 23-26, 73, 159, 237
recognizes   24
recommend   117, 124, 150
record 259
recorded   142, 246
recording   1, 260
records   61, 119, 247, 261
recourse   259
recovery   53
recruiting   230
recurrence   209
redefine   23, 33
re-design   71
reduce45, 48, 153, 156, 216, 228
reducing   99, 127
references   258, 267
reflect 67, 94, 153, 157
reform 51, 112, 124
reforms23, 49
refuse 230
regarding   112, 122, 181, 222
Register   2, 5, 135, 199, 203-204
regret 86
regular37, 42, 73, 250, 252, 258
regularly   29, 151, 219
regulatory   23
reimbursed   234
reinforce   187
reinforced   139
reject 144, 218
rejecting   144, 173
rejection   259
relate 65, 225

related 16, 50, 62, 93, 151, 186, 248, 264
relating   186
relation   25, 82, 123
relations   110
relative 95, 237, 244
relatively   128
release 159, 212, 264
released   223
releases   252
relevant   40, 49, 74, 93, 105, 185, 198, 217
reliable 37, 210
reluctance   238
remain 33
remaining   177, 183
remunerate   80
renewal   251
repair 215
repeat 131, 138
repeatable   205
rephrased   10
replace   54, 256
replanning   157
replicate   188
replicated   257
Report 6-7, 85, 101, 142, 165, 221, 232, 244, 252, 266
reported   151, 157, 159, 246, 249
reporting   65, 95, 119, 144-145, 151, 157
reports 48, 94, 135, 144, 159, 193, 250
repository   159, 212
represent   87, 185-186, 256
reproduced   1
reputation   116
request   6, 61, 185-186, 223-226
requested   1, 223, 226
requests   211, 223
require 35, 51, 68, 70, 96, 98, 134, 158, 170, 177
required   22, 29, 31, 38, 40, 64, 78, 80, 101, 132, 136, 138,
142, 161-162, 171, 189, 217, 219, 230, 263-264
requires   131
requiring   135, 261
research   16, 104, 109, 150, 165, 173, 206, 266
reserved   1
reserves   215, 247

reside 89, 181
resolution   74, 80
resolve 24-25
resolved   180
resource   4-5, 143-144, 163, 169, 171-172, 180, 197, 211,
215, 219, 221
resources   2, 8, 22, 26-27, 37, 43, 51, 71, 78, 95, 101, 115,
117, 125, 131-132, 136, 140, 146, 152, 161, 163, 171, 183, 186,
232, 235, 240, 242-244
respect   1
respond   138, 204, 250
responded   12
responding   204
response   16, 23, 95-98, 101, 217, 252
responses   87, 115
responsive   184
result 81, 87, 150, 183, 197, 200, 226, 261, 263
resultant   214
resulted   100
resulting   62
results 9, 34, 40, 65, 75, 77, 79-80, 82-83, 85-86, 90, 96, 101, 163,
174, 182-183, 187, 211, 214, 220, 239, 242-243, 254, 259
Retain 104
retained   60
retaining   173
retention   53
retrospect   122
return 81, 108, 201, 206
reused 207
revenue   20, 50
revenues   46
review 10, 40, 67, 144, 168, 185, 216, 229, 238
reviewed   39, 198, 229, 251
reviewer   236
reviews151, 159, 206, 211, 216, 258
revised 69, 100
revisions   214, 261
reward 52, 54, 221
rewarded   26
rewards   100
rework 45, 52
rights 1
rigorously   229

routine 97
rushing 240
safety 107
samples   188
Sarbanes   106
satisfied   125, 144, 233, 254, 263
satisfies249
satisfy 132
satisfying   120, 213
savings33, 49, 54, 69
scalable   89
scaled 160
scenario   32-33, 220
schedule   3-4, 41, 56, 99, 138, 140, 142, 156, 159-160, 173,
177-179, 186, 194, 201, 203, 211-212, 223, 225, 246, 252
scheduled   215, 219, 246
schedules   150
scheduling   159, 180, 197
scheme   98
science   73
Scorecard   2, 12-14, 219
scorecards   100
Scores 14
scoring 10
screening   189
scripts 152
seamless   113
second   12
section 12, 27, 43, 57-58, 74, 91, 103, 128
sections   187
sector 248
securing   56, 120
security   18, 73, 79, 100-101, 135, 152, 225
segmented   38
segments   33, 113
select 63, 95, 258
selected   84, 183-184, 206
selecting   65, 114, 234
Selection   5, 213, 236
seller   182
sellers   1
selling 165
senior   119, 128, 187

sensitive   33
sequence   162, 168
sequencing   124, 139, 179
series   11
servers 219
service 1-2, 8, 48, 77, 79, 87, 101, 104, 133, 150, 165, 185-186,
221-222
services   1, 34, 50, 52, 105, 107, 118, 136, 220, 229, 234,
252, 255, 261
serving 230
session 145
setbacks   60, 62
setting 111, 121, 247, 251
several 62
severely   71
severity   203
shared 100, 183, 228
sharing 81, 97, 245
shifts   17
short-term   201, 206
should 8, 18, 24, 26, 32, 35-36, 42, 48, 53, 60, 63, 69-70, 73, 75,
80, 83, 93, 96, 106-107, 112, 120, 124, 126, 128, 131, 135, 138-139,
153, 161-162, 164-165, 173, 175, 186, 189, 191, 196, 207, 213-214,
220, 223, 226, 232, 239, 246, 250-251
-should 185
showing   138
signature   105, 258
signatures   170
signed 251
signers 262
silent   235
similar 29-30, 59, 65, 90, 143, 163, 185
simple 128, 193, 236, 248
simply 9, 228
single   106
single-use   8
situation   21, 44, 177, 242, 248, 257
situations   93
skeptical   115
skills   18, 25, 74, 119, 123, 132, 159, 165, 186, 219, 237, 244-245,
250
sliding 137
slippage   205

smallest   22, 81
social   115, 210, 236
societal   125
software   22, 145, 173, 202, 205, 207, 215, 219-220, 223, 229, 252
solicit   31
solution   61, 74-76, 78-79, 84, 86-89, 92, 150, 152, 210, 252-253
solutions   51, 77, 82-84, 87, 90
solved 24
Someone   8
something   120, 153, 208
Sometimes   51
source 5, 112, 126, 153, 181, 210, 213, 258
sources   37, 60-61
special 31, 96, 217
specific   9, 20, 39-40, 64, 109, 152, 163, 165, 168-169, 177, 179, 195, 212, 222, 225, 237, 256-257
specified   127, 157
specify 157, 245
spoken 123
sponsor   21, 142, 151, 180
sponsors   17, 219, 232
spread 94, 100
stable 201, 251
staffed 43
staffing 18, 99, 140
staffs   238
stages 142
standard   8, 101, 169, 252
standards   1, 10-11, 92-93, 103, 179, 187-189, 191, 225, 230, 247, 258
started 9, 168
starting 10, 139
startup 134
start-up   233
stated 114, 124, 146, 195, 258, 264, 266
statement   3, 11, 76, 82, 143-144, 150, 152, 182
statements   12, 27, 40-41, 43, 58, 67, 74, 91, 103, 128, 192, 251
static   224
status 6-7, 70, 142, 151, 156, 159, 194, 198, 221, 223, 232, 248, 252, 266
statutory   179

steady 46

steering 153, 180, 198, 212

stocks 260

storage 192

stored 230

stories 34

strategic 46, 95, 105, 128, 198

strategies 77, 95, 112, 127, 138, 143, 218, 227-228, 239

strategy 24, 28, 49, 78, 86, 89, 101, 109, 112-114, 125, 143, 263-264

stream 54, 63, 118, 128

strengths 153, 165-166, 214, 234

stretch 121

strict 63

strive 121, 173

Strongly 11, 16, 28, 44, 59, 75, 92, 104

structure 3-4, 89, 120, 128, 154, 171, 177, 179, 212, 217

structured 121, 179

structures 244

stubborn 105

stupid 123

subdivided 193

subject 9-10, 36, 145

subjects 60

submitted 225

subset 22

sub-teams 239

succeed 56, 105, 166

success 21, 30, 35, 37-38, 43, 46-47, 57, 77, 86, 94, 104, 106, 108, 113, 118, 123, 153, 167, 181, 201, 222, 227, 242-243, 263, 266

successes 118

successful 72, 77, 88, 94, 110, 119, 132-133, 138, 171-172, 181, 199, 219, 222, 240

succession 93

successor 159

sufficient 158, 220, 230, 266

suggest 223

suggested 101, 185-186

suitable 250

supervisor 234, 238

supplier 83, 107, 231

suppliers 32, 64, 68, 119, 160, 258

supplies 179, 254
supply 46, 258
support 8, 26, 72, 79, 94, 118, 127-128, 132, 134, 147, 159, 169, 202, 211, 217, 227, 229, 234, 238, 252
supported 69, 147, 201
supporting 80, 99
supportive 195
supports 234
surface 101
SUSTAIN 2, 76, 104
sustaining 98
symptom 16, 50
system 10, 42, 61, 65, 102, 111, 119, 145-147, 153, 156-157, 159, 172-173, 187, 193, 195, 201, 225, 227, 229-230, 239, 247-249
systematic 50, 246
systems 65-67, 71, 77, 81, 99, 137, 142, 180, 214, 216, 220, 229-230, 248, 254, 260
tables 153
tackle 50
tactics 227-228
tailoring 239
taking 50, 174, 221
talent 70, 119
talents 119
talking 8
tangle 194
target 40, 107, 190
targets 121, 248, 257-258
tasked 101
teamed 235
teaming 213, 234
technical 90, 132, 138, 146, 152, 173, 206, 213
techniques 74, 109
technology 54, 85, 101, 104, 132, 165, 173, 201, 206-208, 230, 235, 251
templates 8-9
tenders 259
testable 39
test-cycle 191
tested 27
testing 83, 146, 187
themselves 245
theory 98

things 77, 117, 206, 212, 242, 256
thinking   76, 108
third- 79
thorough   79, 226
threat 19, 110
through   63, 73, 119, 205, 228
throughout   1, 63, 106, 173, 265
tighter 115
time-bound   40
timeframe   164, 183
timeline   225, 243
timely 18, 90, 132, 180, 194, 224, 235, 265
together   104, 259
toilet   230
tolerances   85
tolerated   175
tomorrow   95, 126
top-down   93
topics 90, 142
touched   147
toward99, 221
towards   74
traceable   194
traced 152
tracked   207
tracking   36, 95, 150, 159, 177, 179, 187, 212
traction   115
trademark   1
trademarks   1
trained35, 201
training   19, 22-23, 60, 64, 78, 96, 99, 141, 217-218, 221,
235, 238-239, 266
trainings   22
Transfer   12, 27, 43, 58, 74, 91, 100-101, 103, 128, 252
transition   107, 145
translated   39
travel 235, 259
trends 64-65, 73, 85, 117, 136, 210
trigger 77, 85
triggered   159-160
triggers76, 160, 185
triple   215
trophy 121

trouble 114
trying   8, 230
turnaround   164
typical 219
ubiquitous   115
ultimate   127
unclear   32
underlying   83, 156
understand   39, 131-132, 144, 234, 250
understood   81, 86, 119, 205
undertake   70
undertaken   215
underway   133
uninformed   124
unique 128, 165
universe   250
Unless 8
unpriced   247
unresolved   169
updated   9-10, 67, 142-143, 211, 258
updates   10, 100, 252
updating   143, 160
upfront217
up-sell 113
up-to-date   258
urgent 223
usability   88, 111
usable 194
useful   81, 92, 154, 174, 266
usefully 10, 22
UserID 165
utility   176
utilized 174, 251
utilizing 84
validate   248
validated   35, 39, 41, 59, 63
Validation   248
Validity 147
valuable   8
values 119, 137, 187, 210
variables   97
variance   6, 156-157, 174, 236, 246-247
variances   156, 159, 194, 246

variation   16, 34, 60-61, 99, 160
variety 87
various 142
vendor 131, 167, 180, 198, 259
vendors   20, 65, 79, 160
verbally   193
verified 10, 35, 39, 41, 63
verify   46-47, 49-54, 56-57, 93, 96, 102, 150, 239, 249, 261
verifying   44-45, 54-55, 151
version 252, 267
versions   32, 36
versus 144
vested 112
viable 77, 155
virtual 239
vision   119
visualize   162, 176
voices 135
volatile 90
volume   194
volunteers   234
warning   159-160
warranty   1, 215
weaknesses   143, 166, 214
website   223
whether   8, 99, 117, 196, 231, 265
-which 206
widespread   94
widgets   185
windfall   142
window   164
within   70, 88, 162, 175, 195, 210, 216, 222, 225, 235, 246, 255
without 1, 12, 104, 106, 139, 147, 160, 225, 259, 261
workdays   203
worked   181
workers   122
workflow   68, 227
workforce   18, 85, 113, 119-120
working   98-99, 138, 195, 228
Worksheet   4, 175, 183
worst-case   32
writing 148, 193
written 1, 159, 229, 251

yesterday   17
youhave   145, 177
yourself   111, 115, 196

Printed in Great Britain
by Amazon

40880386R00179